A NEW TONGUE /
LATE STYLE OVID
RICHARD BLEVINS

SPUYTEN DUYVIL
New York City

To Boleslaw Boczek in Ohio

Mightier than the pen or penis   my mind is
—Alice Notley, The Speak Angel Series.

Monday. Me. Tuesday. Me. Wednesday. Me. Thursday. Me.
—Witold Gombrowicz, Diaries.

Since there is no practical difference between the past and the present
and everything is happening today, Ovid must have read Joyce
—Jacek Bocheński, Naso the Poet.

…life is at the transitions
—William James, "A World of Pure Experience."

How long can I let my mind molder in this place?
—C.P. Cavafy.

In the history of art, late works are the catastrophes
—Theodor Adorno, Essays on Music.

EXORDIUM

The nose knows—Jimmy Durante.

I FIRST READ TRANSLATIONS of Publius Ovidius Naso's poems from exile in late fall 2015, for company and instruction, when I moved out of the connubial home shortly after retiring from teaching. I had encountered the *Metamorphoses* and *Art of Love* at college nearly half a century earlier. Now, about to enter a dark period when I found myself afraid of living alone, I read Ovid's *Tristia,* the *Black Sea Letters,* and *Ibis*—not love poems or the poetry of pure reference, but the Ovid of lamentations, pissing-into-the-wind epistles home to Rome, and the diatribe (a new voice for him, and modern-sounding to me) against an enemy not to be named. It was a prolonged period of mourning, worst for me at dusk, which did not kill but panicked. I became smitten by Hermann Broch's *The Death of Virgil*, a book undertaken in a concentration camp and revised in self-exile. Turning my back on writing poetry, abashed by my books of love poems, I finished a novel, my first, started before the breakup and wrote three more. I wrote like Ovid from the inside out, the circumscribed love poet creating frosty novels in which the season is always winter. I waited eight years to attempt my own poem on Ovid, or the span of Ovid's time in Tomis before his death. I have benefitted from something like the arrangement Caesar made for Ovid's wife (she is never named), Martha Koehler lives on in the house, and we remain best friends. I wrote this longpoem with no living Gaius Octavius Augustus in mind. My poem is ambient political, although the leadership's hollow espousal of "social values" may seem familiar today. May the Florida hypocrite tyrants meet in a hell of their own making. It amazed me to know literary conspiracy theorists have been bowdlerizing Ovid for a long time. Some critics, beginning with Herman Frankel in 1945 and repurposed by O. Janssen and A.D. Fitton Brown, go so far as to postulate that Ovid stayed in Rome to write his last books, that Tomis is a fiction like Malouf's virtual novel *An Imaginary Life.* How the poet would laugh to know his readers still mistake the artful narrative voice for him, as Augustus did. See Niklas Holzberg and Michael J. Mordine for Ovid's complex narrative technique; John C. Thibault for the what facts we think we know about Ovid's exile.

Fact is, the longer you look at art, it changes shapes—that is the very nature of art. You can never have all the facts: Picasso's bicycle seat and handlebars look like a statue of Minotaur sometimes when we blink. Ovid changes into a poet we hadn't recognized before: the poet of the autofiction *Tristia*, the *Letters from the Black Sea* littoral, and the howl *Ibis* had already achieved and abandoned a poem of pure reference with the *Metamorphoses*. In one letter from the barbarian frontier, he encloses for Maximus what he calls "pens from Tomis," a quiver of Getan arrows for display on his Roman walls. Twenty centuries after Ovid's death, the Pontus Euxinus is a resort destiny.

The *magnus scolaris* on the relegation is Jo-Marie Claassen. Among the best depositions of Ovid's case is Joseph Skvorecky's in *An Inexplicable Story*, a novel! (Ovid laughs last.) Another novel, Jacek Bochenski's *Naso the Poet,* employs a coded language of state investigation that extends the political tradition of Ovid's method. Ovid claims he learned a new tongue to write a poem in Getic, although he must surely have learned to get by with a little local Greek and hand gestures. For my study, I have made do with David Green's extensive notes to *The Poems of Exile* (which read like an "Ovid and his times"), David Slavitt's translation, a Latin dictionary which survived my ex's high school, and bedtime YouTube of Ovid in Latin—activities directed by a growing sense of Ovid as the first modern poet. I purchased a wax writing tablet on eBay. My project is a sustained poem, more enthusiastic than scholarly. My goal would be to (re)invent Ovid, after Vico's sense of *inventio.* To accomplish more would require another lifetime of devotion approaching Professor Claassen's surpassing love of Ovid. To get as far as I have, too often required breaking the second line of the elegiac couplet into shorter syllable counts, less invention than concession to English. (Pound called his method "translating" Propertius. The same Pound who, in *Guide to Kulture,* says offhandedly that the *Metamorphoses* is Ovid's longpoem. And then Allen Shawn, the composer, emails that he has finished the work of "transcribing improvisations," which is a fair descriptor for my project. What follows are transcriptions into poetic lines my improvisations after Ovid and his commentators.) Among the poetic liberties this non-historian takes concern Ovid's major sources of angst: I intentionally confuse the two Julias, and Augustus for Ibis, making two monstrous nemeses.

The enigmatic conditions and limited resources of Ovid's exile changed Rome's Celebrity Poet into Ovid Circumscribed, an unlikely spokesperson in the age of artificial sources of intelligence. However, his *Ibis* invents the longpoem curse that might prepare the modern reader for Cendrars' obsessiveness or Thomas Bernhard...The *Heri* is an experiment in persona that took form much later in Hazlitt's *Liber Amoris* or Landor's *Imaginary Conversations*...The three exilic books mount an assault on the elegiac tradition that projects beyond Seneca and Cicero into the possibility of Pound's *Pisan Cantos*. Late style Ovid is alienated to a fine poetic madness like Lorca's in New York...They say Ovid's grave is lost, but I know his ashes rest easy in Cocteau's tomb along the ancient Roman road to Lyons...The gap between Ovid's ancient world and our mutating sense of the apocalypse is bridged, in a time when Americans are re-texting bundles of birch rods and axe; when the world's grandest empire has been governed by a hypocrite autocrat, a brute staring down Mors, whose domestic program demanded a "return" to "family values." After Augustus banned the bookrolls, Romans prized ur-samizdat Ovid.

Thanks to the Ovid project, I have come to see Robert Duncan's transformative Grand Collage as a process resembling the making of mosaics from Ovid's longpoem.

FIRST ELEGY

LINES TRACK PEDETEMPTIN PROGRESS
  PROLIX BY SHAPE CHANGE:
RACKET OF AN EMPTY CART
  BOUNCING OVER COBBLESTONE.
BIG NOSE IN SUCH RICH SUN-RICH ROME
  SURELY WAS A BIG
MAN-ABOUT. EX PONTO, I GROW
  SMALLER, LETTER-SIZED:
SHREWSHRINK
  IN THE FREEZER.
THOUGH THE STORY TELLS ITSELF,
  MAXIMUS PERSISTS.
"WHAT DO YOU DO, QUID AGIS?
  FOR FUN I MEAN,
WHEN YOU ARE NOT PLOTTING
  THE OVERTHROW
OR SEDUCING SOMEONE'S WIFE?"
  I GROW HAPPY
IN MY HOMEWORK; I GROW A BEARD;
  I SCRAPE THE PELTS CLEAN
AS A PRETORIAN'S BLUE JAW.
  I WOULD NO MORE
CUT MY HAIR
  THAN MY WRISTS.
I'D SHAVED THE TEENAGE FUZZ
  ONCE OR TWICE BEFORE;
AT EIGHTEEN, I PRONOUNCED MYSELF
  A LOVE-POET.
ALL BLACK SEABASS ARE BORN FEMALE
  AND COOK UP WHITE
  AS MY OLD HEAD.

WHO WOULD MISS YOUR SWARMING STREETS,
   DERALICT BEGGARS,
VETERANS IN HOBNAIL SANDALS,
   STORIED VAGABONDS,
PICKPOCKET ARTISTS AND SICK WHORES,
   THICK AS BOTTLE FLIES
MAKING THE DEAD HORSE
   LOOK ALIVE?
MOVING DAY, THE LOVE-ARTIST'S BED
   WAS TOO BIG
FOR THE GOATSHED. I HAVE THE HUT
   ALL TO MYSELF,
SINCE MY LAST SLAVE RAN OFF
   MUMBLING TELES.
THE CRONE WHO MADE THE DAY'S MEAL
   ACTS UNSIBYLSIZED.
NOW THEY FEED ME ON RUMORS,
   JUST ENOUGH
TO KEEP ME ALIVE. I SWALLOWED
   A TOOTH IN MY SLEEP,
ANOTHER DENT IN MY IMAGE
   DOESN'T TRANSLATE WELL.
LIKE PLEURISY'S REBARBATIVE
   SPEAR IN MY RIBS,
IT WON'T KILL ME, ONLY MAKES ME
   SHORT-WINDED
FOR A PUBLISHED POET.
   I PANT
AS IF RECOVERING FROM SEX,
   WITHOUT THE PLEASURE.
FINE EUXINE WINE MORPHS OVERNIGHT
   INTO THE SHAPE
   OF MY BOWL:
I CUT OFF SLICES OF THAT FRUIT,

PERICARP
    FOR BREAKFAST.
"TO CUT," THE GREEK WORD FOR TOMIS,
    NEW CUTCITY,
MEANING I AM CUT OFF FROM YOU.
    MISS EVERYBODY.
NEED A HAIRCUT SO YOU WILL STILL
    RECOGNIZE ME,
MAKING IT HARDER TO MISTAKE
    ME FOR MY POEM.
NEVER TAKE HEROIC FOR
    EROTIC COUPLETS.
    MAKE NO MISTAKE:
I STRAINED AGAINST THE LIMITATIONS,
    "WHATEVER I TRIED
TO WRITE WAS POETRY."
    APPLES CANNOT GROW
FROM THIS BLOODY GROUND, I KNOW,
    IT WAS NEAR THIS POST
MEDEA KILLED AND THEN BUTCHERED
    HER BROTHER
TO DELAY HER PURSUERS.
    HIPPOMENES
    CAN NEVER WIN
THE RACE TO LOVE, AND PARIS
    WILL NEVER JUDGE.
THIS TRYING TO JUGGLE FOUR APPLES,
    ALWAYS KEEPING
    ONE IN THE AIR,
IS GETTING ME DOWN. THE POET
    IS CURSED
    BY REFERENCES:
DRUSUS CHOKED ON A PEAR
    HE THREW IN THE AIR.

EVEN IN THIS BOOKLESS STATE,
   PALAMEDES
    COMES FOR YOU.
  TOMIS! TO THINK, I FIRST MISHEARD
    ITS NAME
    FOR TEMENOS!
"I GIVE YOU YOUR LIFE—I CAN TAKE IT TOO,"
    MEDEA TO JASON
    FROM MY LOST DRAMA;
SHE INSTRUCTS PELIAS' DAUGHTERS,
    GO CUT UP YOUR FATHER,
    DRAIN AWAY OLD BLOOD!
THE PLAYWRITING EXPERIENCE
    MADE ME A NEW MAN.
DO I SOUND SO DIFFERENT?
    DURING MY SIXTH YEAR
    OF EXILE,
I COMPOSED A POEM IN GETIC
    AND RECITED
    TO MY HOSTS.
IT IS MY GREATEST
    METAMORPHOSIS
    TO DATE.
I ROUGHLY TRANSLATE MYSELF
    FOR THE MARKET SQUARE:
OVID, OF ALL KNIGHTS, HAS BECOME
    NECESSARILY
A SOLDIER AND A FARMER
    IN A SHORT
    GROWING SEASON.
I WRITE TO SPITE HOME-SPUN VERGIL,
    WHO PLOWS FURROWS
ALONG POLITICAL LINES.
    "VERGIL DOES NOT

SO MUCH PREDICT CHRIST
   AS ROBERT FROST,"
HIS VOICE IN THE NIGHT SPOKE NONSENSE,
   NAMING THE WEATHER
AND THE CRIMINAL
   CO-CONSPIRATORS?
(THE FORM OF AN APPLE, THE FORM
   AN APPLE TAKES,
IS NOT HOW THE APPLE FORMS.
   DOWN THE "STYLE,"
POLLEN ENTERS THE OVARY;
   FERTILIZED,
BLACK SEEDS ON THE OUTER WALL
   BECOME WHITE FLESH;
SEEDS ON THE INNER WALL BECOME
   THE APPLE'S CORE.
FROST CAN BLEMISH THE NEW PEEL
   CAUSING UGLY
SCARF SKIN OR RUSSET.)
   UNHAPPY
IS THE MAN WHOSE FLOOR
   IS DIRT;
HIS TEARS MAKE MUD,
   NOT LYRICS.
I SEE THAT DULL STYLUS PULLED
   BY OXEN,
   DEFECATING
ACROSS TABLETS IBIS GAVE HIM
   FOR RETIREMENT.
ARISTAEUS, HIS BEEKEEPER,
   MISTAKES THE KING
FOR THE QUEEN BEE IN HOT PURSUIT
   OF EURYDICE.
   THE QUEEN DOESN'T MOVE.

MY SOLE CONCESSION TO VERGIL
   COMES IN "CURES FOR LOVE,"
ON DIVERTING THE LOVESICK MIND
   WITH HARD FARM WORK.
ALAS, FIELD LABOR DID NOTHING
   THAT ENNOBLED
   MY CITIFIED ASS
WHEN IBIS SENT ME TO PASTURE
   IN THE TUNDRA.
AS FOR HORACE, RETIRED
   TO THE SABINE FARM
   THANKS TO MAECENAS,
I HAVE ONLY CONTEMPT. STOP.
   THERE IS NEWS—
IBIS, I AM ONLY SORRY
   I CANNOT RETURN
FOR YOUR FUNERAL.
   I AM ON MY KNEES
BEFORE YOU, ASKING FOR NOTHING
   FOR ONCE.
WHEN WE NO LONGER BELIEVE,
   GODS BECOME STORIES.
AND YET, DECKHANDS CRY OUT
   TO THE DEITIES
AT THE FIRST SIGN OF LIGHTNING,
   QUICK TO WRAP THEIR ARMS
AROUND SOME PAINTED IDOLS,
   AND CLING TO THE POOP
AS OUR HELMSMAN FLINGS HIMSELF
   OVERBOARD.
DIONYSUS WOULD HAVE TURNED THEM
   ALL INTO FISH.
THE COLD YELLOW SUN BECOME
   A LEFTOVER EGG

COAGULATED ON A PLATE,
   WE MADE LAND.
"MY LIFE IS RESPECTABLE;
   MY MUSE
TELLS THE DIRTY JOKES." I QUOTE
   MYSELF FREELY
A BOOK ISN'T EVIDENCE,
   IT'S ALL FUN AND GAMES.
"I AM WAITING FOR THE SENTENCE
   TO BE REVISED."
   ALL GIGGLES AND FARTS
LIKE GALIO'S BAN TO LESBOS:
   A PAID VACATION.
BUT CAESAR IS DEAD AND I HAVE
   ZERO CHANCE
WITH LIVIA. I'VE ALREADY
   RIGGED UP
AN ALTAR FOR HIS BIG EXILE,
   WHERE I BURN
SMALL SACRIFICES OF MY SELF-
   CENSORSHIP.
I RECEIVE HIS STANDARD
   REJECTION SLIP.

SECOND ELEGY

THAT NIGHT IN THE MARKET SQUARE,
     I SANG THE PRAISES
OF AUGUSTUS, TIBERIUS,
     LIVIA, AND GERMANICUS,
PAUSING ONLY FOR VINEGAR
     AND PLANT ASH
"PUELLA DOCUIT ME MELOQUI."
     READ THE LAUDIO
LIKE A TRANSLATION OF YEARNING
     LETTERS HOME.
STILL LEARNING THE WEST COAST MYTHS,
     I SERVED UP
A THIN STEW OF GETIC AND STREET
     GREEK—
MY MALNOURISHED AUDIENCE
     LAPPED IT UP;
THEY CLAPPED, STAMPED THEIR BOOTS, AND FARTED
     IN APPLAUSE…
LUCKY FOR ME ("WHAT THEY DON'T LIKE,
     THEY KILL."),
THEY DON'T MAKE SENSE OF GOD'S BODY
     REPOSING
ON THE PALATINE AS HE IS
     ASCENDED
INTO THE GODHEAD. I GUESS I
     LOST THEM BACK THERE,
WHEN I PRAISED CAESAR'S BELLY
     TO THE SKIES:
I POINTED OUT THAT HIS BIRTHMARK
     APED THE GREAT BEAR…
AUGUSTUS IS THE NEWEST STAR

IN THE CONSTELLATION,
    FAR BRIGHTER THAN ALIOTH,
        I TOLD THEM
    I FOLLOWED TO THE LETTER
        HIS "LEX JULIA
    MARITANDIS ORDINIBUS"
        —I,
    THE ONLY ONE OF HIS POETS
        (SOLUS)
    TO MARRY, MUCH LESS THREE BRIDES.
        ONCE FOR EVERY TIME
    HE LOCKED THE DOORS TO TWO-FACED
        JANUS' TEMPLE. HELL,
    FAMED NAMES HORACE, AND VIRGIL
        (NICKNAMED "VERG-INAL")
    NEVER WED. I GAVE THE STATE FULL
        APOTHEOSIS,
    WHEN ALL I'D NEEDED WAS A NOD
        OF HIS HEAD,
    THE LIFTING OF HIS RINGED FINGER,
        OR THE ARCH
    OF HIS UNIBROW
        —*TO BE RELEASED.*
    MY CONCOCTION FILLED THEIR BELLIES
        WITH ROCKS FOR A PYRE
    TO AUGUSTUS, WHO IS ALWAYS
        IN THE ROOM.
    THEN FOR DESSERT, I RECITED
        "ON FISHING"
    IN THEIR NATIVE TONGUE IN SAUCY
        DIALECT.
    MAYBE ONE OF MY BEST READINGS,
        CERTAINLY THE ODDEST:
    I FELT "A MEAGRE JUICE REACHES MY

EMACIATED JOINTS
AND MY LIMBS ARE PALER THAN NEW WAX":
   MAIMED BY WOUNDS
   THAT DO NOT KILL.
EVEN WHEN MY KNEES GAVE OUT,
   I SURVIVED
LIMPING IN ALTERNATING FEET
   TREE TO TREE,
OFTEN RESTING; PROPPED WEAK LEGS
   ON A CRUTCH
WHITTLED FROM A LIMB OF PONTIC
   IDIOMS
AND ADYNATON I'D GATHERED
   FROM THE GRAFTED ELM—
"UNLESS I MAKE LIXUS FLOW
   INTO THE HEBRUS,
AND ATHOS ADD ITS LEAVES TO THE ALPS,"
   NONSENSE LIKE THAT.
MY PRONOUNCED LIMP MAKES ME GO
   IN CIRCLES.
OTHER LINES GO TOO LONG TRYING
   TO CATCH UP.
TO PAD MY PRAYER TO AUGUSTUS,
   I PLAGIARIZED
WHAT I KNEW BY HEART FROM MY OWN
   ARS AMATORIA,
(THE BOOK THE IMPERATOR
   HATED MOST!)
AND FILLED IN BLEMISHES WITH LINES
   ON LADY'S MAKEUP.
AGAIN, THE GETS SHOOK THEIR QUIVERS
   IN APPLAUSE
AND MURMURED STRANGE APPROVAL.
   AFTERWARDS,

I TOOK QUESTIONS
    FROM TOW-HEADED HOSTS—
TZARA, FATHER OF ZIA, ROSE
    TO ASK HIS:
"YOU LOVE CAESAR SO MUCH,
    SURELY
HE CAN'T HELP BUT CALL YOU BACK!"
    TURNS OUT,
THE BRUTE'S A NATURAL CRITIC.

ALL CRITICS WRITING
AFTER HOMEROMASTIX
   THE HOMER-WHIPPER
ARE BRUTES. TIME I STOP
   MINCING ABOUT
FLATTERING IBIS, AND ACCEPT
   MY FATE.
I HADN'T MADE IT CLEAR TO THEM
   AUGUSTUS IS DEAD.
TOO BUSY KISSING ROYAL ASS,
   I MYSELF REMAIN
UNCLEAR HOW TO DESCRIBE
   HAZY AFTERLIFE:
MAKE CAESAR SKIP ANTIUM,
   FOR A CHANGE,
AND SUMMER IN CUTCITY HELL.
   BUT THE GARRISON
IS PLEASED TO FREE ITS POET
   FROM PAYING TAXES
FOR AS LONG AS I MAY LIVE.
   (THEY PUT A FREE HORSE
AT MY DISPOSAL IN ROME,
   RENEWABLE.)
JUST DO NOT EXPECT POEMS
   UPON REQUEST
FOR YOUR BIRTHS, DEATHS,
   MARRIAGES, FESTIVALS,
ANNIVERSARIES, AND WARS OR GODS
   AS YOU HAVE THEM.
(BRINGS TO MIND THE "TAX PAID" TATTOO
   ACROSS THE SLAVE'S BROW;
AND SOMETIMES THE OWNER'S
   INITIALS.)
TO PLEASE MY HOSTS, I WORE

ON MY BROW
THE SACRED RED BANDANA
   THEY BESTOWED.
MY HONORS NOW EXTEND,
   LIKE A BOOKROLL,
THE BREADTH OF THE PRESENT EMPIRE.
   GROWN LIKE A NEW CULT,
MY HONORS EXCEED
   MY ACCOMPLISHMENTS.
BRUTUS STANDS READY
   TO BANKROLL
A METAMORPHOSES SEQUEL.
   GOOD THING
THESE PUTRID BEASTS CAN'T READ LATIN—
   IF THEY EVER DO
DECIPHER MY LETTERS TO ROME,
   THIS CHEERING MOB
WILL HAVE MY HEAD, THOUGH I'M INNOCENT
   AS CINNA.
THEY CARRIED ME HOME ON THEIR SHOULDERS
   DEAD DRUNK
(PRAISE WENT TO MY HEAD.)
   DEAR POLLIO,
MY RECENT SUCCESS UNCOVERS
   A PRESSING NEED.
ROME'S LIBRARY SHOULD GROW
   A THIRD WING:
ONE FOR THE GREEK BOOKS,
   ONE FOR THE LATIN,
AND GETIC IN BETWEEN.
   I LONG TO FLY
ON THREE STRONG WINGS
   ABOVE THE BORDERS
AND PAST THE ESTATE
   TIBULLUS LOST.

THIRD ELEGY

THIS MARKS MY SIXTH WINTER
   AMONG THE GETS.
ALL THIS TIME, I HAVE HEARD
   NEITHER TIBIA
   NOR CITHARA.
ONCE I SANG TO PATRICIANS,
   BACKED BY CRACK
MUSICIANS. AN EXILE WRITING
   DANCES IN THE DARK.
I STOPPED FLATTERING MYSELF
   RIGHT ABOUT THE TIME
PROBOSCIS STOPPED TELLING HIMSELF
   YEARS AGO
THAT I WAS THE LOVER
   IN THE POEMS.
I RAISED FASHIONABLE SAILS,
   SET OUT UPON
SO MANY FALERNIAN SEAS
   ONLY TO WIND UP
BLISTERING MY PRETTY HANDS
   ROWING FOR MY LIFE.
THERE ARE SPIDERS, BIG ONES,
   WHO DON'T PLOT WEBS;
THEY RUSH THEIR VICTIMS
   OUT OF NOWHERE!
THE WOLF SPIDER HIDES BEHIND
   ARCHITECTURE,
POUNCES WITH OBSEQUIOUS
   DELIVERIES
OF EPISTLES HE DARES NOT READ,
   SOME SERVILE

TABELLARIUS SUCKLED

    ON SHE-WOLF LORE.

THINGS AREN'T SO BAD HERE.

    DON'T EXAGGERATE.

I WASN'T SENT TO AORA;

    THE MOSQUITO

IN MY EAR IS NO BIGGER

    THAN A PIG.

I PROUDLY WEAR AROUND MY WRIST

    THE VELATA

    CORONA.

I PRAY YOU, SPREAD MY ASHES

    BY THE GATE

I ONCE GUARDED WITH MY LIFE.

    I TRY TO MAINTAIN

GOOD HABITS:

    I BRUSH MY TEETH WITH URINE

RELIGIOUSLY.

FOURTH ELEGY

WHAT STRANGE BIRD BURSTS INTO THE ROOM,
  FLYING BACKWARDS,
EXHAUSTED AGAINST HIGH WINDS?
  I'M AFRAID
TO APPROACH—SHE MAY BE OMEN,
  OR GODDESS
SACRED TO THE BARBARIANS.
  I SEE IT MOVES
ONLY BY STICKING OUT ITS NECK
  REPEATEDLY
TO DRAG ITS BODY.
  IT HAS NO FEET.
TRANSFORMED, THE AUTHOR OF *IBIS*
  FIRST DARED
THE ART OF LOVE THEN, QUICKLY,
  THE CURE FOR LOVE:
TWO SCORPIONS DANCE IN BARE-FOOT
  ORION'S BEDROOM,
THEIR PINCERS EMBRACE EACH OTHER,
  THEY MATE.
I NO LONGER COUNT ON CLUES
  FOR METRICAL MOVES
BY READING FACES OF LOVERS
  OF POETRY.
 AUGURY IS BAD POETRY,
  CORNIFICIUS.
AROUND HERE, ACOUSTICS ARE SO BAD
  MY VOICE RETURNS
SOMEONE ELSE'S TO MY EARS,
  MORE REFLUX THAN ECHO.
ATTICUS WAS MY FIRST READER;

NOW WE ARE CUT OFF.
SOMEWHERE I WROTE
   "IN FELIX, QUOD
NON ALTER ET ALTER ERAS."
   (WAS IT *FASTI*?
OCTAVIUS WAS VESTAL PRIEST
   WHEN HE CUT IT OFF.)
THE POEM SHOULD INCLUDE
   EVERYTHING, MYRIS,
IF I START MAKING CUTS
   IN COUPLETS,
IT WON'T BE LONG BEFORE THE WAX
   IS RUINED.
I ALWAYS TRUSTED MY STYLUS
   TO CUT THE RIGHT WORDS
IN THE ORDER IN WHICH THEY COME
   TO ME.
YOUNG OVID AGREED WITH FRIENDS
   HE'D ELIDE THREE LINES
IF FIRST HE COULD ELECT THREE LINES
   SACROSANCT:
IN THE EXCHANGE, ALL HAD SELECTED
   THE SAME THREE LINES.
THAT WAS BEFORE IBIS ORDERED
   NIGHTS TO LAST LONGER,
EVEN AS VENUS HASTENED HIS
   CORONATION DAY.
THE MAN'S SPRUNG FROM A FAMILY
   OF EQUITES!
SINCE HE BECAME IBIS, A NAME
   WRITTEN IN CRAP
ON THE WALLS OF PUBLIC TOILETS,
   EVERY DAY
I WORK ON A LIKENESS,

A MONUMENT
  TO CAESAR SALUTING THE CROWDS
    FROM HIS ASS,
  SCULPTED FROM MEMORY
    IN MY OWN TURDS.
I MAY BE BURNING DUNG FOR HEAT
    IF WINTER PERSISTS.
ALL THE ROOTS AND BRANCHES
    I COULD GATHER
MADE LITTLE SMOKE OFFERINGS
    WEEKS AGO.
THE DOGS SLEEP INSIDE WITH ME;
    THE PALATINE SLEEPS
INSIDE ME FOREVER.
    THE UNFRIENDLY SUN
THINS, CALDA ON ONE
    HORIZON FOREVER.
IT SPILLS WITHOUT WARMING
    THE BODY.
RAIN ALWAYS BRINGS TO MIND
    THE BODY…
IT IS DECEMBER AGAIN.
    UPROOTED,
I LEFT HOME IN DECEMBER
    O, THE FLOWERS
I DID NOT GET TO TEND
    AT CLODIA WAY!
SPRING COMES LATE HERE
    OR NOT AT ALL.
LATE SPRING
    WHEN I ARRIVED.
AT THE RUMOR OF SPRING THE TUNDRA
    BRAIDS ITS PUBIC HAIR
IN FLOWERS WHICH NO MAN PLANTED.

SINE SEMINE FLORES.
EVERY FOURTH TENEBROSUS
    IN EVERY WEATHER,
I TAKE MY TURN ON THE WALL,
    ONE OF TWENTY
SILLY SOUP KETTLE HELMETS.
    GAIUS JULIAS
WOULD HAVE ERECTED A TOWER
    WITHIN THE WALL,
LIKE THE ONE FOR HERCULES
    AT PUNTA EUROS,
SO AT LEAST WE COULD SEE THEM
    COMING.
STANDING GUARD, I DAYDREAMED
    A VISION:

TIBERIUS HAS PLANNED A TRIUMPH FOR MY HOME-
COMING, A CELEBRATION
OF MY REBIRTH. ACKNOWLEDGING THE MANY GODS
I'VE CAPTURED OR KILLED OUTRIGHT.

HE HAS THEM IN WORKSHOPS MIXING THE RED LEAD
PAINT FOR MY FACE JUST RIGHT.
SEE, THE LICTORS ARE OUT IN FRONT, WALKING
AHEAD OF ME, CRYING "GETOUTTHEWAY!"

AND "MOVEYOURASS! OVID IS COMING!" WE PROCESS,
STAGED STEP BY STEP, THE POET
WHEELS INTO VIEW ON HIS FOUR-MAN LITTER (MY
COUCH SEDAN FOR COMPOSING LOVE)

BRAVELY ENTERING A STORM OF ROSES THROWN
ONTO THE PATH OF HIS BLOODLESS TRIUMPH
(MY FEET NEVER TOUCH THE GROUND) OF COURSE,
MY UNPOLISHED EXILIC POEMS,

THE SPOILS OF WAR, ARE ON DISPLAY AT THE FORUM AU-
GUSTI. MY PROCESSION
TAKES ITS GOOD TIME DOWN THE VIA SACRA AS IF SHOP-
PING, PAST VESTA'S SHRINE

AND NUMA'S OLD PALACE, THROUGH THE PORTA MOGUNIA
AND UP THE PALATINE
SKIRTING THE TEMPLE OF JUPITER STATOR AND ON TO AU-
GUSTUS' PALACE,

HIS GOLDEN-WREATHED DOOR MISSING THE FLOWN EA-
GLE, ADJACENT TO APOLLO'S TEMPLE
(I MET CORINNA THERE, UNDER THE DANAIDS) THENCE
BESIDE THE TIBER TO THE CAPITOL,

WITH BRIEF STOPS FOR HURRAHS AT THE PORTICO OF OC-
TAVIA, THE THEATRE OF MARCELLUS,
THE HALL OF LIBERTY. THE ONES WHO GAVE ME UP FOR
DEAD, ARE CONSPICUOUS

OF COURSE, THEY CHEER THE LOUDEST BOTH SIDES OF THE
STREET, THE CROWD WANTS A PIECE OF ME

AT LENGTH WE ARRIVE AT THE FORUM, WHERE EVERY-
BODY IMPORTANT OR WISHING TO BE SEEN

HAS HAD TO WAIT IN LINE TO KISS MY SORRY ASS PASSING.
(LOW SOUNDS OF WORKMEN

BUILDING THE EXTRAVAGANT TOMB FOR MY NAME STICKS
HER TONGUE IN MY HAIRY EAR)

THE COST OVERRUNS THREATEN TO RUIN IBIS (THE
ANSWER TO WHO IS BURIED

IN OVID'S TOMB), ALWAYS THE PRIME SPOT FOR PICK-
ING UP GIRLS.

   SHAGGY AND SOOTY,
IF I SUDDENLY SHOWED UP
   UNANNOUNCED,
I'D FRIGHTEN OFF THEM ALL BUT ONE,—
   EVEN MY WET NURSE
WOULDN'T KNOW ME, FOR MY SCAR
   IS INTERNAL.
MY POEMS HAVE ROUGHENED TOO—
   ALL BUT FABIA.
THE NETS THE GET FISHERMEN CAST
   SOMETIMES CATCH MONSTERS,
LODGED IN THE HOLES BETWEEN WORDS,
   BAD POETS THROW BACK.

FIFTH ELEGY

KNOW THAT YOUR DAUGHTERS ARE SAFE WITH ME
   (AND POSSIBLY THEIR MOTHERS).
WILD NIGHTS ON THE ROSTRA
   CANNOT WARM MY ARMS.
ITS ROSTRUM IS REBUILT WITH WOOD
   FROM THE TWO JUNK PILES
THAT DEPOSITED ME HERE.
   WHEN I COULD HAVE
RETURNED, I DISEMBARKED
   FROM THE "HELMET,"
WHOSE FIGUREHEAD WAS ARMORED
   MINERVA.
SPEED-READING ELEPHANTIS'
   FOOD PORNOGRAPHY
ROTS HOI POLLOI FROM INSIDE OUT,
   BUT NOBLE GUTS
YET ENTWINE IBIS' VEINY LEGS
   CAUGHT JUST WITHDRAWING
FROM THE ORGY HE'S ALREADY
   PUBLICLY DENOUNCED.
ALL THE GARUM IN THE HOUSE
   WILL NEVER MAKE
THIS COLD DISH SAVORY.
   I AM CAST AWAY
FOR A SONG AND AN ERROR,
   PULLED LIKE A TOOTH
FROM IBIS' ROTTING MOUTH.
   THE KING OF NAPLES
NEVER MADE A LAW WITHOUT FIRST
   SENDING IT PAST ME.
I PLEADED AN ADVOCATE'S CASE

IN THE *TRISTIA*.

FEARLESS CICERO WARNED, LAW IS

    THE MIND OF GOD.

DO NOT MISTAKE ME FOR

    MY CRUMBLING SMILE.

I AM MUCH YOUNGER

    THAN I FEEL,

MY COMPLEXION LOOKS

    LIKE A PILE OF LEAVES.

NASO'S NOSE WAS CUT OFF AND HE

    FOUND IT IN HIS BREAD.

THE BREATH OF THE BARD FREEZES

    HIS BEARD.

ADULTEROUS FUCKTARDS HAVE LEFT

    MY TOMB

A MATTER OF CONJECTURE!

    AM I SPEAKING

CLEAR SARMATIAN?

    YOU WILL FIND

THE LOST AUTOBIOGRAPHY

    DE VETULA

SEALED IN THE AIRLESS SEPULCHER,

    A FAVORITE FAN

ALWAYS WITHIN HER REACH. MY MIND

    OBSESSIVELY

RETURNS TO THE UNFINISHED TASK,

    TANTALUS

IN WATER UP TO HIS BALLS.

    CORINNA'S FAN

UNFOLDED, A CIRCLE OF STICKS,

    EACH STAVE

IS THIRTEEN INCHES LONG—

    SAXICOLINE

KORE GROWS FROM ROCKS—THE DOCTOR

PRESCRIBED
DREAMS FOR BAD INSOMNIA,
   SENDING OPIUM
CUT WITH TINY YELLOW PEDALS
   GLAUCIUM
FOR ME TO MIX WITH THE LOCAL
   BRACKISH WATER.
IT ALWAYS MAKES ME DREAM
   THAT I'M ASLEEP, I COMPARE
   THE STAGES
OF SEDUCTION TO ROOMS
   IN MY WIFE'S
   COMMODIOUS HOUSE,
FABIA LEAVES OPEN THE DOORS
   INTO DEEP SLEEP,
WHERE VIRGINS LIGHT INCENSE
   FOR THE GODS,
I BURN STRAW AND DUNG
   FOR WARMTH.
ANIMALS DEVOUR THE NIGHT,
   FISHBONES I TOSSED OUT.
THEY BURY ALIVE LAPSED VIRGINS...
   THE RELEGATION…
BREATH BY LOG LIGHT MAKES THE COLD HUT
   SHIMMER.
"EVERYTHING I WRITE..." UNTOUCHABLE
   WALLS OF MOSAICS…
IMAGINE MYSELF SNUGGLED
   BENEATH THE GOLDEN
FLEECE THAT COCKY JASON CARRIED
   OVER A SHOULDER
INTO CUTCITY, MEDEA
   SPEAKING HER LINES
TO JASON IN THE PLAY

I TOSSED OFF FOR HER…
BY FAR, THE ROOM'S BIGGEST OBJECT
   IS THE BOOKROLL,
THIRTY FEET OF GLUED PAPYRUS,
   I'M WORRIED,
THIS ONE TAKES TWO SLAVES TO CARRY
   TO THE WAITING SHIP.

Sixth Elegy

CRUEL TO WAKE

    STILL ALIVE

[...]

    KNOWING

[...]

    LOVE HAS DROPPED

ME HERE, A PIECE OF MEAT CIRIS

    THE CUTTER LOST

ON THE ROCKS FROM HER BEAK.

    BECAUSE DOVES REFUSE

CARRION, I HAVE LEARNED

    TO LIVE APART,

BUT NEVER WITHOUT YOU, ROMA,

    OR THE HOUSE

THAT IS MY THIRD WIFE'S,

    AS CAESAR DECREED.

I SEE CORINNA HAS ADDED

    A TATTOO

TO HER CHARMS, PLUS THAT PHILISTINE

    HUSBAND OF HERS.

MY EX-WIVES LEFT NO TRACE.

    EVEN MY STEPPE-

DAUGHTER PERILLA

    HAS GIVEN UP ROME.

SHE WRITES POEMS IN AFRICA

    COOLED BY

THE CELEBRITY WATERFALL

    SHE CALLS HER HUSBAND.

ALL WATER HERE IS FROZEN STIFF.

    OUR ONLY STATUE,

LAODAMEIA'S DEAD CONSORT,

LUNA MARBLE
SILENT BEFORE PAINTING, AWAITS
   SPRING BURIAL.
ROME NEVER GETS OLD,
   CUTCITY
NEVER GETS NEW. NO STREETS
   TO SECRET,
FREEZING TO DEATH
   ATOM BY ATOM
MEMORIZING THE *GEORGICS*.
   I WAS WRONG.
I HAD FAILED TO IMAGINE
   A PLACE
PAST CHANGING. THROUGH EIGHT LONG YEARS,
   NOTHING HAS CHANGED.
ZENO WAS WRONG: ACHILLES DID
   CATCH THE TORTOISE,
AND MADE HOT SOUP.
   THANKS!
I WROTE THE POEM OF PURE REFERENCE
   YET I AM CONTROLLED
BY HE WHO MANIPULATES MYTHS
   LIKE NEWS,
THE ABSENT ONE WHO IS
   NEVERTHELESS LAW
IN MY LOATHSOME STATE OF WAITING
   FOR THE NEXT ARROWS
   TO LAND.
NASO'S BANISHMENT LEAVES *META*
   AN ABANDONED NAP,
MY TRICKLE PERSIFLAGE BECOME
   A SNORE NEXT DOOR.
WRONG, WRONG. ALL SONG AND ERROR.
   LEAN CLOSER, IBIS,

AND ZENO WILL WHISPER THE NAMES
   OF KO-CONSPIRATORS.
I HAVE BITTEN OFF MY OWN TONGUE
   AND SWALLOWED,
CUT A CROW'S TONGUE
   TO MAKE IT TALK.
I AM COMPLICIT, I ADMIT,
   I WAS THAT PUPPET
TO THE FUNNY PERSONA
   I CREATED.
ONTO WAX TABLETS, I POURED FORTH
   THE BLASPHEMY
THAT A SLAVE TO LOVE ACTUALLY
   MEANT SOMETHING.
"CAN IT REALLY BE A CRIME
   TO ERR?"
I CONFESS I SEE MY NIGHTMARE SELF
   RIDING JULIA
TO THE FINISH THE VERY INSTANT
   I SPY IBIS
FUCKING A LADY UP THE ASS
   LIKE SHE WAS THE EMPIRE.
THE REST IS ANCIENT HISTORY.
   SEX IS A RHYTHM,
   A BEATING PULSE,
IT TAKES A REAL POET
   TO SUSTAIN.
BODIES GET TRANSFORMED
   IN THE PROCESS.
(BECAUSE OF A WORD, THE VOLANT LINE
   DIGRESSES,
A STONE'S BEEN TOSSED INTO THE BAT'S
   FLIGHT.)
AS I WATCHED, JULIA SWALLOWED

THE PRIEST'S TOOTH

AND GAVE BIRTH TO THE CHILD TO BE

   BRAINED ON THE HILL

TO THE SIGHS OF THE CITY

   DIDDLING TO CLIMAX.

BUT I NEVER ONCE JOINED IN.

   THE PUBLIC BATHS

   ARE NOT FOR BATHERS.

THE POET'S SONG SEDUCES

   BUT LEAVES NO HEIRS

LIVIA'S BEHIND THIS, STILL PISSED

   I SAW HER FLABBY ASS,

WHILE IBIS WATCHED HER FUCKING

   OUR EYES MEET

WITHOUT A WORD, EURYDICE

   VANISHES, POOF.

STICKING MY BIG NOSE IN WAS

   A BUSINESS ERROR.

(CAN ARGUS BE SURE HE'S SHUT

   EVERY EYE

ON HIS BODY? POETS SHOULD SEE

   EVERYTHING DOUBLE.)

WELL, IT'S HIS HOLIDAY AND HIS MONTH

   ON HIS CALENDAR.

MAY THE REINSTATEMENT OF SALUS

   MAKE ROME GREAT AGAIN.

WITHIN TWO YEARS, EVERY CAT IN THE ALLEY

   WAS YELLOW.

I NEVER MADE IT AS FAR AS AUGUST

   IN MY *FASTI*.

BY THE TIME THE SNOW COVER MELTS,

   HARD AS A ROAD,

IT'S WELL PAST SPRINGTIME

   WORMWOOD.

THE CHILD CANNOT CROSS THE NEW RIVER
    TO CONTINUE
MY EDUCATION. WE SEEM
    TO HAVE TAKEN SIDES.
WHAT, I WONDER, COULD BE HER WORD
    FOR PONS?
I WAKE GASPING FOR AIR TRAPPED
    UNDER RIVER ICE.
I CAN SEE UNREACHABLE LAND
    ABOVE ME, IN DREAMS
I AM CHOKING TO DEATH, DYING
    SEVERAL
SUCCESSIVE AGONIZING DEATHS,
    PALINURUS
FALLING OVERBOARD INTO MIRRORS
    CLOSING OVER ME.

SEVENTH ELEGY

DON'T KNOW FROM WHENCE HE CAME
    BUT I HAVE A PET.
HE COMES TO THE NAME VERGIL,
    AND ALSO RESPONDS
TO THE FIFTY GREEK NAMES OF
    ACTAEON'S CANUM.
I CAUGHT VERGIL STEALING FISH
    AND DROVE HIM OFF.
NEXT DAY, HE TURNS UP AND STAYED.
    GETS USE THEIR DOGS
FOR HUNTING, HERDING, GUARDING CAMP,
    FISHING, AND BETTING.
VERGIL RECALLS MY FORMER SELF,
    DISAPPEARS FOR DAYS…
JUST WHEN I GIVE HIM UP FOR DEAD,
    HE SHOWS UP
ON THE DOORSTEP IN BAD SHAPE,
    STARVING FOR FOOD;
HE SLEEPS THROUGH THE NEXT TWO DAYS,
    THEN WE'RE PALS
ALL OVER AGAIN.
    GUILT HAUNTS ME.
MY CHILDHOOD DOG GREW BLIND
    AND SELDOM STIRRED
FROM BED, MY FATHER CARRIED HIM
    DEEP INTO THE WOODS.
THE VERY WORST PART IS NEXT.
    AFTER FOUR BLOWS,
THE YELPS STOPPED. I HAD WANTED
    THEM TO STOP.
PYTHAGOROUS ONCE STOPPED A MAN

BEATING HIS DOG.
HE'D RECOGNIZED A DEAD FRIEND'S VOICE
IN THE YELPING.

Eighth Elegy

I WALK INTO A SPIDER'S WEB
   I SWEAR
WASN'T THERE A MINUTE AGO.
   NASO PREDICTS,
ONE DAY NASCENT CUTCITY
   WILL BE
A JUMPING SPIDER WHO DEVOURS
   HER MATE.
THE NOSE KNOWS. AS VERGIL'S WEB CAUGHT
   OVID, SO MINERVA
CONTROLLED THE NARRATIVE OF
   THE MAJESTY
OF THE GODS, CHANGED ARACHNE
   INTO A SPIDER
THUS CENSORING THE BETTER WEAVE
   DEPICTING
GODS RAPING WOMEN. TEREUS
   CUTS THE TONGUE
BUT FREES THE SONG. JULIA WEEPS
   THAT SHE IS GIVEN
ONLY THE THREE MORTAL HOLES
   FOR FUCKING.
THE CITY'S BEST-SELLING POET
   SQUATS IN WORMWOOD
AND SHITS AMONG FLIES,
   WHO ONCE LAPPED HIS WINE
FROM PATRICIANS' RIMING PAPS.
   JULIA'S GRANDPAP
HAS RULED THAT EVERY SINGING THRUSH
   BY THIS DATE
MUST TURN INTO A TURD.

CAESAREAN BIRTH
IS A CUT BY LAW THROUGH THE DEAD
MOTHER'S MUSCLES.
BEST AVOID SWAMPS, PROLIFIC
VARRO WARNS PEOPLE,
WHERE DISEASES ARE KNOWN TO THRIVE,
MULTIPLYING
GENERATIONS OF FETID GETS.

Ninth Elegy

REFINED TIBULLUS,
I REMIND YOUR SHADE
   WHAT YOUR BODY KNEW
   ONLY TOO WELL:
KOAN SILK IS BY ITS NATURE
   DEMURE—
SEE HOW IT FILLS IN
   BETWEEN HER KNEES,
WHICH BY ART YOU HAVE WORKED OPEN
   A LITTLE BIT. ZONA,
HER BELT IS A TRIP TO THE ZONE
   ABOVE THE DANUBE'S
IRON GATES. THE REST WAS EASY—
   UNDOING
HER NOT-NOT KNOTS
   THEN
A FEW CLASPS TO NAVIGATE.
   BUT THE BRA,
FASCIA REQUIRES A MORNING
   TO PASS BENEATH
   A WHISP OF CLOUD.
I HAVEN'T FOUND A FARMER'S WIFE
   PLEASED TO ALLOW ME
   TO LIFT
THE HEAVY BURDEN OF HER BREASTS.
   DULCEM.
THE GET GIRL'S FEET ARE BEAUTIFUL
   IN HER "RED CLOTH-WRAPPED
LEATHER BOOTIES…TRIMMED IN TIN,
   PYRITE CRYSTALS, GOLD FOIL
AND GLASS BEADS SECURED WITH SINEW.

FANCIFUL SHAPES…
DECORATE THE SEAMS." THE GIRL'S LEGS
    ARE ALWAYS DIRTY.
OLD HAND QUICK TO STRIP THE YOUNG WIFE
    FALLEN THROUGH THE ICE,
WRAP HER IN FURS FIT FOR A NEW
    CORRINA
(WRONG SIDE OUT, WARMTH OVER BEAUTY).
    I'VE PUT ON
TOO MANY LAYERS
    TO FLOAT—
LAYERS OF DEFENSE, LAYERS
    OF MEANING—,
IF I FALL IN, I'LL SINK FAST
    TO THE BOTTOM.
NO USE TRYING TO SAVE ME,
    I'LL PULL YOU DOWN TOO.
DOOR SLAMSTARTLES ME AWAKE—
    I'D DREAMED
I WAS FREE AGAIN TO GO
    WHATEVER DIRECTION
MY ERECTION POINTS. YOU LEFT
    WHILE I NAPPED,
I DIDN'T GET TO SAY GOODBYE.
    THINKING THIS
IS THE EMPIRE'S DAY FOR PRAYER,
    I HAD TO HUSTLE
LIKE ACHILLES TAKING UP ARMS
    AND RUSHING OUT.
IN THE CONFUSION WHEN THE GUARDS
    CAME FOR HIM,
POUNDED IN HIS DOOR, THE POET
    HAD TIME TO GRAB
CONFUCIUS AND A JAMES BIBLE.

(THESE TERMS ARE NOT
FAMILIAR. THESE ELIDES
    MUST BE THE FUTURE.)
LUCKY THEY DIDN'T SLAY HIM
    ON THE SPOT.
IN THE CAGE, HE WROTE A CANTO
    MAKING THE FOUR
FAITHFUL FRIENDS IMMORTAL STARS
    OVER ITALIA:
BRUTUS, CARUS, CELSUS,
    ATTICUS.
TOSSED OVERBOARD, I SURVIVED
    THE TENTH WAVE
BY CLINGING TO A NEW FRIENDSHIP
    JUST FLOATING BY
WITHIN GRASP AND NO SHIP IN SIGHT!
    WASHED UP
LOVE'S PRECEPTOR HAS A BUDDY.
    ONE MAN'S INCEST
IS ANOTHER MAN'S INNOCENCE,
    BUT CAESAR
IS A GOD NOT AN INCENSED MAN.
    MAY I OFFER UP
THIS NONSENSE INCENSE IN THE FORM
    OF APOLOGY?
SORRY I NEVER MADE IT THROUGH
    THE WHOLE "LEX JULIA,"
ONLY SKIMMED IT LIKE CELSUS'
    ENCYCLOPEDIA:
I AM LOOKING FOR WHAT AILS ME.
    MORE MOSQUITOS
THAN STARS LAST NIGHT IN THE GREAT BEAR'S
    FIRMAMENT.
I WILL STAY IN BED TODAY.
    MAYBE SHE DROPS BY?

TENTH ELEGY

WHEN I WASN'T LOOKING
   MY BEARD TURNED WHITE
AS A SACRIFICIAL BEAST'S
   GRIZZLED BRISTLES.
WHEN I CHECK THE BOOKROLL,
   IT'S "HIRSUTUS SPARSIS
UT UIDEARE" TOO!
   AND YET,
THE SCROLL IS SCENTED ON THE BACK
   WITH CEDAR OIL,
AND ROLLED AROUND AN IVORY ROD,
   SECURED
WITHIN ITS RED SLIPCOVER.
   A BOWL OF WATER
WAS MY ONLY MIRROR. IT GLOWED
   WHITE AS IVORY
PYGMALION CARVED, THE WHITENESS
   OF COOKED SEA BASS,
WHITE AS VERGIL'S BELLY FUR,
   MELIAN WHITE
CONTRIVED FROM MOLLUSK SHELLS.
   WHEREVER I LIVED,
MY DAYS WERE CRAZY BUSY
   MAKING NOTE-POEMS—
STRAY LINES ROUSED ME NIGHTS
   TO LIGHT THE LAMP
TO LAY A PHRASE. I WILL BE DEAD
   SO LONG,
WHATEVER WILL I DO
   WITH ALL THE TIME?
FROM THE END OF THE LINE, I SEND

MILLE TRECENTI
LINES A YEAR. YOUR OVID STILL WRITES,
    DELIBERATELY,
AS IF LATIN WERE HIS GREEK.
    ALL MY CASH
IS BRONZE TOMIS COINS.
    TODAY MARKS
MY SEVENTH MARCH XX
    IN CUTCITY.
A PRISONER NEVER WISHES
    TO REPEAT A DAY.
I COMPOSED IN SEVERAL SITTINGS
    A CALM LETTER
    TO MY WIFE
(ONLY THE ONE BITTER PASSAGE
    ON IBIS) TO SWEAR
I REMAIN A FAITHFUL AND CHASTE
    VEGETARIAN
STARVING FOR THAT SLIM CHANCE,
    TEMPTATION
IN THE AIR, SMOKE FROM ROASTING PORK;
    THREE MORE POEMS
DISGUISED AS EPISTLES TO FRIENDS
    LEFT BEHIND
(ONE TO THAT BASTARD); A LOVE NOTE
    TO CORINNA. WAIT!
SEBINUS' LETTER'S DELIVERED—
    RIGHT ON TIME
    FOR WIPING MY ASS.
ONE DAY, I SWORE OFF EATING MEAT
    THE REST OF MY LIFE.
DIES NATALIS MEANS TO MAKE
    A START, DOESN'T IT?
I SPENT THE BIRTHDAY ENJOYING

NEWFOUND SELF-CONTROL,

ESCHEWING CAKES AND INCENSE,

NO LIBATIONS,

NO TURF ALTAR OR LAUREL WREATH,

NO WHITE GARMENTS

SINCE I RETURNED INO'S VEIL

DIRECTLY

INTO THE HOSPITABLE SEA,

LETTING NO ONE KNOW

ALL DAY IT WAS MY DAY.

THE WOMAN-SLAYER

NASO BECOME UGLY

AS THERSITES.

SOMETHING MORE THAT'S HARD TO SWALLOW.

SOMETIMES WHEN I EAT,

MY THROAT CLOSES, AND I MUST FORCE

MYSELF TO THROW UP.

IN THE OLD DAYS, I VOMITED

SO I COULD EAT MORE!

WORDS FOR POEMS RISE UP LIKE GALL

FILLING MY MOUTH.

I'M LOSING WEIGHT FAST. MY LIMBS GROW

STIFF WITH GOUT.

THE PRECIOUS STONE HAS FALLEN

FROM MY WEDDING RING.

MY TEETH EVICTED GOLD. I BURNED

MY ROTTED TOGA.

LIKE ANY GOOD SAVAGE,

I WEAR PANTS;

I SMELL OF SMOKE AND DAMP SHEEP'S WOOL.

ROMANUS VATES,

I PASS FOR A MOTLEY GET,

AS LONG AS

I KEEP MY MOUTH SHUT. THE DIRK

    MANICURES

LONG NAILS. I EAT SITTING UP.

    I SHOULD BE HAPPY

FRIENDS CAN'T SEE THE LIFE OF THE FEAST,

    AND MY ENEMIES

CAN'T POINT ME OUT. I'M WARNING YOU,

    SWEET FABIA,

I'M QUITE THE PRIZE.

ELEVENTH ELEGY

EVERY LOVE STORY TELLS ITSELF.
   PROLIX BY CHANGE, NEW
LINES RECORD THE LOVER'S PROGRESS.
   NOSTRIL SHRINKS DAILY,
THE SHREW IN THE FREEZER.
   I STAY HOME NIGHTS
DURING THE RELEGATION MONTHS,
   THE MOTH ESCHEWS
MY WRITING LAMP WHOSE FLAME
   IS NO GOOD
FOR EITHER OF US. THE MOTH
   IS NOT NATIVE,
HE CAME IN ON THE BOAT WITH ME.
   I HAVE COME TO PACE
THE BEACH WHEN THE WIND BEATS
   LIKE A MAD ROMAN
RECITING LOVE ELEGIES
   INTO SPACE,
SMATTERINGS OF GETAN, GREEK,
   AND SARMATIAN
DRIBBLE DOWN MY FACE.
I LIVE LIKE SOMEONE'S ANCESTOR.
   I SAW VERGIL ONCE
BUT COULDN'T FIND MY TONGUE.

THE STORY I PROMISED   COMES NEXT.

LIKE A BREAK IN THE WEATHER
   THE GIRL ARRIVED
CARRYING MY WATER ON HER HEAD.
   BEFORE LONG,

I WILL HAVE A NEW TONGUE
   THANKS TO THE KID
PUELLA DOCUIT ME LOQUI.
   FROM HER MOUTH,
GETAN IS MORE THAN GRUNTS AND CRIES
   OR THE ORAL FARTS.
SOON I WILL BE EMPOWERED
   TO THINK THE POEM-
GIFT FOR HER CHIEFTAIN FATHER
   IN A NEW TONGUE
FOR A NEW WORLD! GOOD FRIEND STRABO
   TENDED TO FALL OFF
MAP'S END MID-SENTENCE…
   "I AM ZIA,"
SHE MAKES ME UNDERSTAND, "I AM
   'ONE WHO FEEDS THE HORSES.'"
"GRAIN" IS YOUR NAME IN LATIN,
   I LAUGH. SHE'S PUZZLED.
I INDICATE MINE BY TOUCHING
   MY NOSE
AND REPEATING "NASO."
   NOW WE HAVE NAMES.
THE MASTIFF LISTENS, FEELS SAFE
   TO CLOSE HIS EYES
IN THE WARMTH, WHERE ZAFTIG ZIA
   AND SHAGGY NASO
WEAR OUT THE SUN WITH TALK,
   INVENTING CHEEKY
EPIGRAMS THAT PILLOR THE LIVES
   INSIDE THE WALL,
THE MIGRANT AND SULPICIA.
   ALONE WHEN I WRITE,
WADING INTO THE ENDLESS STREAM
   AGAIN, COLD WITH MELT

FROM PEAKS OBSCURE TO ENEMIES.
  I FEEL SECURE
KNOWING THE RAIDING PARTIES
  CANNOT CROSS OVER
THE BRIDGE OF ICE AT THE DANUBE
  AND STEAL THE FORGED FISH
OUR FARMER'S PLOWS DISCOVERED,
  OUTSIDE THE WALLS,
HIDDEN IN FIELDS IN COCKEYED ROWS.
  THEY LOOK DOWN IN AWE,
INSTEAD OF OVER BENT SHOULDERS
  FOR THE NEXT ATTACK,
OR WINTER. THEY CULTIVATE
  MONUMENTAL STONES.
MEANWHILE, I JUST PLOW THE BEACH,
  KILLING TIME,
SOMETIMES IN THE SHADE OF MYRON'S
  CUD-CHEWING COW OR
  CALAMUS' HORSES,
IF NOT WALKING BESIDE RIDERS
  LIKE YOUNGER CATO.
ALL VILLAGERS RIDE EVERYWHERE,
  CARRING LONGBOWS
AND ARROW SHEATHS, EVEN IF IT'S
  JUST AROUND CABIRI
  TEMPLE, AND BACK.
THEY RACE SWIFT AS PODARGOS—
  PEDESTRIANS BE DAMNED.
YOU CAN SMELL THEM COMING
  BEFORE YOU HEAR
THEIR RESOUNDING HOOVES NEARBY.
  LETHAL IS
MY PROTECTERS' SMELL, MORE SMELLY
  AND LESS DEADLY

EVEN THAN PHILOCTETES' FEET.
   ALL THE BOYS
ARE FECKLESS PUNKS IMAGINING
   THEMSELVES GROWN MEN;
THE MEN IMAGINING GIGANTOMACHIANS,
   ARE MANY TIMES WORSE.
THEY BRAY AND SHOW THEIR BLACK TEETH
   LIKE THOSE HORSES
THAT LOOK FOR A CHANCE TO THROW
   THE RIDER.
THEY ARE HORSEMEN BRED FROM THE MARES
   OF DIOMEDES,
WHO HATH FED ON HUMAN FLESH.
   ANIMAL INSTINCT
INFORMS THEM THAT, IN A PINCH,
   THE MASTERS WILL EAT
THEM BEFORE STARVING. I MYSELF
   COME FROM EQUITES
AND CULTIVATORS OF LEISURE.
   SLOTH IS VICTORIOUS
WITHIN UNFALLEN WALLS CAVING
   IN ON THEMSELVES.
EVEN ZIA SADDLES A HORSE
   TO FILL MY CUP
WITH MARE'S MILK. THIS NEW LANGUAGE
   I'VE PICKED UP
IS UNFIT FOR ORATORY
   OR PILLOW TALK.
IT SEEMS DESIGNED TO BE HEARD
   ABOVE DRUMMING HOOVES,
FROTHING MADNESS, AND THE TRAMPLED
   CRIES FOR MOTHER.
I REALLY SHOULD BURN THIS BOOK
   TO WARM THE ROOM, BUT—

IT MIGHT BE MELEAGER'S LOG.
  THREE THINGS MATTER
IN ANY WRITING: LOCUTION,
  LOCUTION, LOCUTION.
SUCCESS IS ALL IN HEARING
  A DIVINE VOICE.
ONCE, I LET THE HEROINES WRITE
  IN THEIR OWN WORDS
(WHAT HELEN CALLS LITERA
  NOSTRA NOUO),
A NEW KIND OF WRITING THE OLD
  EPISTLE
MAY NOT EVEN BE POETRY.
  TO BE SURE,
THE COUPLET SHAPE REMAINS A BRIDGE
  OVER THE ABYSS.
LEAVING ROME, I BURNED MY OWN
  METAMORPHOSES.
EVERYBODY KNOWS THE REST.
  THE GET GIRL
IS FOREVER STEPPING ON
  THE THRESHOLD;
HER TINY MOUTH WORKS LIKE THE DOOR
  SHE LEAVES OPEN.
NEVER MIND THAT LITTLE BRAT
  OPENLY COVETS
THE THREE BRONZE MEDALLIONS
  MY FRIEND COTTA SENT.
I'VE ALWAYS INDULGED MY GIRLS.
  BUT HOW CAN
A BARBARIAN BE SO SPOILED
  SO YOUNG?
NEVER MIND. NOW YOU'RE HERE,
  WE'LL START.

OUR LESSON FOR TODAY
   IS MANNERS.
ONE DOES NOT STEP UPON THE SILL,
   IT INSULTS US.
ZIA WITH A BIRD IN HER HAND.

TWELFTH ELEGY

PEERING INTO THE POLISHED MIRROR
   OF MY SWORD,
SOMEONE ELSE LOOKS BACK AT ME.
   IN A CERTAIN LIGHT
I SEE MYSELF A SUICIDE,
   NEVER A KILLER.
ONCE A WEEK, I HOLD MY NOSE
   AND GUARD THE WALL
WITH ALL THE STRENGTH OF A GENTLEMAN.
   WHY SHOULDN'T I
TAKE TO MILITARY DUTIES
   NATURALLY, WHEN
THE WOODPECKER MAKES A HELMET
   BY WRAPPING HIS HEAD
IN HIS TONGUE? AESCHYLUS WAS FIRST
   A SOLDIER DRINKING
   VINEGAR.
ARCHILOCHUS DROPPED HIS SHIELD
   AND BOUGHT ANOTHER.
AND I WROTE THAT EVERY LOVER
   IS A SOLDIER
STUDIOUSLY AVOIDING SERVICE.
   LIGHTNING VICTIMS
ARE FINGERED BY AN UNSEEN GOD'S
   THROW OF THE DIE.
FACELESS TERRORISTS KILLING
   OUR SPIRITS
RAIN ARROWS OVER THE WALLS
   AND RIDE OFF.
THE BAD WATER IS KILLING ME,
   EACH SIP

ANOTHER ARROW

IN MY THROAT.

DIE LIKE THE DOG WHEN IT'S YOUR TURN,

TOSS THE KNUCKLE BONES!

I AM THE UNCERTAIN GUARD.

BLONDE AS MINERVA,

OUR FIERCEST DEFENDER

IS DUCCIDAVA.

HER FLOWING HAIR MAKES AN EASY

TARGET WITH BOTH

STRONG ARMS CROSSED BELOW THE BREASTS

IN DEFIANCE.

AND THE WAY SHE CAME IN RIDING

CAMILLA'S SPEAR!

DURING SKIRMISHES,

SHE MAKES ME FEEL ASHAMED,

SNAPS IN TWO

INCOMING ARROWS

AND TOSSES THEM BACK, CICERO

IMMUNE TO POISON.

"BARBARIAN HOST

AT THE BORDERLINE OF SENSE."

SHE BELONGS AMONG

THE ARCHERS IN *TOXOTIDES*.

THIRTEENTH ELEGY

THAT LAST MORNING, SHE RAN OFF
   WITHOUT ME
TO CHECK ON THE THREE SPARROWS' EGGS
   IN THE NEST
WE'D UNVEILED IN THE TAMARACK.
   SINCE I KNEW THE DOG
WOULD LET NOTHING HARM THE CHILD,
   I WENT ON
TAKING PAINS OVER A LETTER
   TO MY WIFE.
VERGIL RETURNED, AFTER DAYS,
   ALONE.
HE SLEPT AT MY FEET WITHOUT EATING,
   AS IF DEAD.
THE GIRL'S PARENTS, QUICK TO BLAME
   THE MIGRANT,
MOVE EVEN NOW TO HAVE ME
   PROPERLY STONED
AT THE GATE, IF TZARA HASN'T
   TORN ME TO PIECES.
MOURNING ORPHEUS CHARMED THE ROCKS
   THE FURIES THREW—
HE GAVE THE BEST PERFORMANCE
   OF HIS LIFE—
WE WILL ALWAYS READ AND WONDER AT
   THE FLOATING HEAD.
IN ANOTHER WORLD, I SANG NUX,
   THE WALNUT TREE
WHO BEGGED FOR HIS OWN DESTRUCTION
   TO AVOID TORTURE.
THE CONSPICUOUS MOURNERS

HAVE SHAVED THEIR HEADS,
SO THEY LOOK LIKE NEWLY ARRIVED
   STRANGERS.
VERGIL HAS ABSCONDED WITH ONE
   OF THE GIRL'S BOOTIES.
I GIVE HIM THE MATCHING ONE
   FOR A TOY.
HIS NOSE DETECTS HER PRESENCE;
   IT IS A BLESSING
FROM THE GODS MY NOSE CANNOT
   SCENT ABSENCE.
HE WILL RETRIEVE THE RED BOOTIE
   AS MANY TIMES
AS I THROW IT.

FOURTEENTH ELEGY

THE BLINDING CIRCLE OF MARBLE,
    WHITE LIKE A PHOSPHENE
SIGNALING A WICKED MIGRAINE,
    AWAITS AUGUSTUS.
BUILT ON A BANK OF THE TIBER
    IN ITS SACRED GROVE
WHERE EVERGREEN TREES FORM A MOUND,
    HIS MAUSOLEUM
HARBORS MARCELLUS, DRUSUS,
    AND AGRIPPA;
FOREVER CLOSED TO BOTH
    THE JULIAS.
CAESAR HIMSELF WROTE *RES GESTAE*
    FOR THE TWIN COLUMNS.
ROUND LIKE A RING FOR A GIANT,
    CREMATORIUM
WHERE THE FINGER SHOULD BE.
    SEEN FROM A DISTANCE,
THE DOME'S BRONZE STATUE OF CAESAR
    LOOKS SMALL AND BLACK.

Mensis Augusti MMXXIII

PARALIPOMENA
To Mircea Cărtărescu

Nothing would be easier than to help a prisoner escape,
if you have, in comparison to him, an extra dimension:
you simply take him between your fingers
and lift him up, perpendicular to his world,
into a pace he cannot imagine—Solenoid.

Colon from *Amores*

HER SLAVE WON'T ADMIT OUR CITIZEN,
    HE SPEAKS WITHOUT.
LO, SOME HAND OPENS THE DOOR
    A CRACK…
ONE SLAT IN THE WOODEN BLINDS
    LIGHTS THE BED.

Catalexis

THE FIRST POEM IN MY FIRST BOOK,
    THE *AMORES*,
STARTS WITH VERGIL'S WORD "ARMA."
    BUT MY CUPID CUTS
A METRICAL FOOT FROM LINE TWO,
    TRANSFORMING EPIC
INTO ELEGIES FOR THE LOVE
    OF CORINNA.

Vergil Reads to Augustus

THE TIME VERGIL READ THREE BOOKS
   FROM THE *AENID*,
HIS DIVINE AUDIENCE OF ONE,
   AUGUSTUS,
NEVER MISSED THE UNFINISHED
   FORTY LINES,
EMPTY AS VERGIL'S HOUSE IN ROME.
   (WHEN THE WINDS SHIFT,
LOOK OUT YOU DON'T GET A MOUTHFUL
   OF BODY ASHES.)
VIRGIL NEVER MISSED A BEAT; POSTMODO,
   CAESAR RETREATS
DAZZLED AND GRATIFIED TO LEARN
   HE HAILS FROM PIOUS
ORIGINS, A BIG FAMILY
   BACK IN A TROY
HE HAS NEVER LAID EYES ON.

   MY FANS ARE LEGION,
CUPID'S NOOSE AROUND THE NOUS.

On Dating (after Pindar)

STROPHE:

EQUESTRIANS GET LOADS OF REQUESTS TO ARRANGE
RACES AT THE CIRCUS MAXIMUS, BUT I NEVER
FOLLOWED THE HORSES OR PULLED FOR A STABLE.

(SEXY ENOUGH, THE RIDE'S ALL OVER IN SEVEN LAPS!)
MY BEST BET FOR HOOKING UP WITH GIRLS WAS ALWAYS
THAT TRACK ROMULUS USED TO DISTRACT THE SABINE.

ANTISTROPHE:

CITIZENS, IF YOU GO TO AVENTINE HILL, GO PREPARED
FOR ADVENTURE. FIRST, RESCUE YOUR GIRL OF THE DAY
FROM THE SMOTHERING CROWD—TRIGINTA MILLE EYES

ARE TRAINED ON A DOZEN CHARIOTS, JUST YOUR TWO LOOK OUT,
ALREADY A PAIR, FOR HER.—COMFORT HER SCREAMS, WRAP BOTH
ARMS AROUND HER WHEN CHARIOTS CRASH (*SHIPWRECK*) TURNING.—

THE DRIVER (CATIANUS!) HAS ALREADY WRAPPED THE REINS
AROUND HIS BODY TO STEER, BY SHIFTING SIDE TO SIDE
HIS WEIGHT: FREEING HIS HANDS AND ARMS FOR THE WHIP

OR DAMNING HIMSELF TO DRAG BEHIND THE FRENZIED ANIMALS.—
(POOR SCORPIUS WAS HALF) THIS GIRL'S AGE, PRAISE PELOPS!
SHE CONSIDERS THE JOCKEYS DECKED OUT IN BRILLIANT BLUE

EPODE:

OR GREEN, REPRESENTING COMPETING STABLES DEDICATED
TO THE SKY AND MOTHER EARTH, AND LOVES THEM EACH.
BE HAPPY TO PLACE SMALL WAGERS, FOR THE PRICE OF A KISS,

ALL AROUND YOUR SEATS FALL SCATTERED SHOWERS
OF COINS, A GENTLE RAIN INTO PALMS. SHE KNOWS
EVERY JOCKEY BY AGE, CLASS, NAME, AND PRIZE MONEY.

SHE GOES CRAZY WITH ANTICIPATION TO SEE THEM
LINE UP IN *PRISONS*.—NOW THE *EDITOR* DROPS HIS MAPPA,
EVERY GATE SPRINGS OPEN AT THE SAME INSTANT, IN-BREATH.—

SUNGLINT OFF WHITE CLOTH AS IF A RAISED BLADE MIRRORED
IN ROW UPON ROW OF WIDENING EYES—EXCITARE, HETAIRA—
    THE START!
IF DIOCLES DOESN'T WIN,
    THE RACE WAS RIGGED—
THE TRAINED SWALLOWS WITH PAINTED LEGS
    WERE RELEASED EARLY
TO SPREAD THE NEWS THAT BLUE HAS WON.
    FROM THE START.
WHILE RACES RAISE GREAT CLOUDS OF HOPE,
    DUST ENVELOPS US.
LONGBOTTOM LOST EVERY BET.
    WE WERE AMONG THOSE
WHO SHOUTED FOR THE JOCKEY'S
    MANUMISSION.
THE NEW RELIGION WOULD RETIRE
    ALL THE GODS FOR ONE.
THE ONE GOD WOULD MAKE LOVING
    CORINNA A SIN.
THEIR SAD WORLD REQUIRES A PROMISE
    (A NICE AFTERLIFE)
JUST TO MAKE THINGS EVEN.

I PUT MY MONEY
ON HORACE, WHO ADMONISHED US,
    CARPE DIEUM
QUAM MINIMUM CREDULA
    POSTERO,
AND LET IT RIDE.

The Best Bestiarius (Just Left the Arena)
I NEVER DID WITNESS THE GAMES,
    MAN AGAINST ANIMAL
OR LION CHAINED TO ELEPHANT,
    WITHOUT THROWING UP.
THE SPECTACLE OF BODIES
    FORFEITING
TRANSFORMATION IS NOT A SPORT.
    IT'S BLASPHEMY.

TenebroCity
LOVERS CAN SEE THE WHOLE CITY
    FROM THE FOOT OF HIS STATUE
BUT THEY ONLY HAVE EYES
    FOR EACH OTHER.
AEDILES SHOULD POST A WARNING
    FOR COUPLES ABOUT
TO DESCEND THE TEMPLE STAIRS:
    "THESE STEPS CONTINUE
UNDERGROUND."

Inside the Pomeriam

SPRING IS UNFATHOMABLE:
    A NAVAL BATTLE
ON A MAN-MADE LAKE WHEN I MEET
    A NEW GIRL.

The Baths of Rome

LET US DRY OFF AND CONSIDER
    THE POETICS
    OF THE BATHS.
THIS SYSTEM FOR MEETING LOVERS
    AND LOVERS MEETING
    GOES ON BEHIND
THE MASSIVE ARCHITECTURE
    AND SEMI-DIVINE
    SCULPTURES.
A LAKE IN THE COUNTRYSIDE FEEDS
    THE INSATIABLE
    CISTERNS OVER OUR HEADS,
WATER TO BE CONSTANTLY WARMED
    IN BOILERS
    FIRED BY WOOD,
PLUS FURNACES THAT FURTHER HEAT
    THE TILED FLOORS
    AND HOLLOW WALLS
WITH HOT AIR, SUCH ARE PROMISES
    BETWEEN LOVERS.
"TO SAY MANY THINGS IS EQUAL
    TO HAVING A HOME."

Love and Music
YOU CAN'T WRITE ABOUT IT
    WITHOUT IT.

The Bikini Mosaic in Casale
THE SECOND COURSE ARRIVES
    ON TIME WITH THE TIDE.
NEW COUPLES RECLINE ON FINE MATS
    WITHOUT EATING,
OBLIVIOUS TO THE POET
    ENTERTAINING,
WAIVING OFF SUPERFLUOUS FOOD,
    AS IF BUZZING GNATS,
UNAWARE OF THE BOUNTEOUS SEA:
    TWO GREEK ISLANDS
APRICATIA UNDER SUN,
    STOMACH-DOWN.

The Martyr
ON THE HEELS OF THE TWO WHITE BULLS
    WITH PAINTED HORNS,
THE DEFEATED PRINCE IN HIS CAGE
    PASSES BY
AT THE HEIGHT OF THE GENERAL'S
    TRIUMPH.
THE DRUGGED PRINCE GETS TREATED BADLY
    BY THE FROTHING CROWD:
HE IS POKED, PROVOKED, AND SPIT UPON.
    AFTER ALL,

THEY HAD TO STAND ON THEIR FEET
   AND WAIT
FOR A LONG TIME IN THE HOT SUN
   FOR A PEEK.
SPECTATORS REMEMBER THE PRINCE'S
   MEMBER
BEING A PES LONG AND PAINTED
   OR TATTOOED.
THE BULLS WILL BE SACRIFICED SOON
   TO JUPITER.
THE PRINCE WILL BE SMOTHERED TO DEATH
   WITH HIS OWN COCK.
SLOW HOOVES OF THE BULLS TRAMPLED
   FLOWER PETALS
STREWN IN THE STREETS BY REVELERS.

Askesis

THE LOVE-POET IS NOT A DRUNK,
   EPICURIUS:
HE NEEDS TO KEEP HIS HEAD
   AMONG THE DRINKERS,
FOR SEDUCTION IS AN ART
   DEMANDING SOBER RESEARCH.
HOSTS DRINK WINE LIKE WATER—
   I NURSE MY WATER
PRETENDING IT'S UNDILUTED WINE.
   I ALWAYS LEAVE
THE BANQUET TABLE
   A LITTLE HUNGRY
BEFORE THE FURIES
   DEFECATE.
MY DECISION TO GIVE UP SEX

SETS ME FREE
FROM THE STRICT FORMALITIES
   OF MATING AND WRITING.
I LIVE WELL WITHOUT TOUCHING
   GIRLS, MEAT, OR STRONG WINE.
I MADE WORDS CHANGE INTO IMAGES
   AND BACK AGAIN.
I REFUSED TO DON
   THE STYLISH WIG.
I LOVED WELL A WIFE
   AND TWO MISTRESSES,
ROME AND POETRY.

Palinode

ALL I REMEMBER, I SWEAR,
   ARE HER FEVERISH ATTEMPTS
AT COOLING HER SWAMPY BOSOMS
   WITH THAT TINY FAN,
ALL THE WHILE IN THE THROWS
   OF A WILTING TIRADE
MOUNTING IMPRECATIONS AGAINST
   HER HUSBAND,
   THE KNUCKLEBONER KNUCKLEHEAD,
WHO LOST THEIR FANCY SUMMER HOME
   COOLY THROWING DICE.
ONE THING MORE: BY THE TIME I'D CUT
   A HOLE IN THE ICE,
I WAS TIRED OF FISHING. OUR SWEAT
   POOLS IN HER NAVEL.
WE ARE FRESH OUT OF GLACIER ICE.
   HER SALIVA
COULD BE A KISS, OR INSULT'S SPIT?

PRESSED, I DO RECALL
CLIMBING THE SLIPPERY MOUNTAIN
AFRAID I'D FALL OFF!
BELOW ME, AT THE FRISSON
WHIMPERING, DAMNING,
PRAYING IT'S EVEN HOTTER
IN HISPANIA,
THE DORMANT VOLCANO RUMBLES
LIKE INDIGESTION'S
NOXIOUS GASSES FROM COSMETIC
BEANS FOR HER TOILET,
AND HEAVES ROCKS EVENTUALLY,
BUT NO LAVA.
OUT OF JEALOUSY FOR THIS ONE,
MY SECOND WIFE,
DIVORCED ME, THE RECIDIVIST,
INTOXICATED
BY MY FANTASY CORINNA,
WHO IS POIESIS.
GREAT ACHILLES, IF YOU CAN HEAR,
PRAY DO SCRAPE
SOME RUST FROM YOUR SPEAR DIRECTLY
ONTO ME.
HIGH TIME FOR HEROIC MEASURES!
I AM THE OPEN WOUND.
MY TOURNIQUET HAS BEEN WOUND
TOO TIGHT, TOO LONG.
LIBRARIANS NEATEN THE STACK
OF MISSIVES DISMISSED,
EACH SHEET OF PAPYRUS IS CUT
FROM MY SKIN:
THE NIPPLES GIVE IT AWAY.

The Critic's A Donkey's Ass
I'M WRITING THIS IN EAR WAX,
    THIS POEM'S SO SLIGHT.
THE MORE I WRITE, THE BETTER
    I HEAR.
FOR HIS MUSIC CRITICISM,
    MIDAS WAS GIVEN
THE LONG EARS OF A DONKEY.

Motion to Reopen
TWO LEAVES OF A WAX TABLET SLAM:
    CASE CLOSED. INSTEAD,
A SOUGHT-ATER POET SHOULD BE
    TRIBUNE TO THE PLEBS,
NO FURTHER THAN A DAY'S RIDE
    FROM THE CITY.

Cut Flowers
ONCE, MY POEMS FOR CORINNA
    WERE FASHIONABLE.
AFTER WRITING, I GREW FLOWERS
    ABSENTMINDEDLY
IN THE BED CARNIVOROUS PLANTS
    HAVE TAKEN OVER.
THE DAY I CLOSED MY HOUSE,
    ONE BIT AT MY HEELS.

Layover in Samothrace
I WROTE THE *TRISTIA*
    BACK IN CORINTH,
IMAGINING THE WINTER
    AHEAD.

On a Poet's Influence
I LIVE IN A REPLICA
    OF ALCAEUS' HOUSE
AND I AM DYING INSIDE
    DENIED NOURISHMENT.
I DON'T DARE DIRTY A CUP—
    JUST PICKING IT UP
WOULD SPOIL THE EFFECT
    I'VE ACHIEVED.

Booked
CAESAR DRESSED ME DOWN IN PRIVATE,
    DREW THE CURTAIN RODS,
SEALED ALL DOORS TO THE POET,
    ACCUSING ME
OF COMMITING POLYMORPHIC
    SEX WITH BOOKS.

Word from Teutoburg

A YEAR INTO MY EXILE,
    CUTCITY ENJOYED
A SPIKE IN POPULATION—
    TWENTY THOUSAND
DEAD SOLDIERS UNDER VARIUS
    JOINED ME.

My Personal Transformation

LATE STYLE IS A NEW TONGUE.
    IT DARES CHANGE PLACES,
ONE WORD FOR ANOTHER,
    ONE ALTERNATIVE
WORLD FOR ANOTHER…HOWEVER,
    THE STALK OF MY TONGUE
RESEMBLES THE SNAIL NOT A LITTLE.

My Plan for the Book

First of all, then, Herodotus, we must grasp
the meanings associated with the word sounds...
—Epicurus, Letter to Herodotus.

WRITING THESE ELEGIESS TAPS OUT
   AFTERHOURS
RESPONSES TO A CODE I HEAR
   FEOM THE NEXT CELL
ON THE DARK WALL OF MY SKULL.
   THE LETTER-SOUNDS
MAKE BOLD PLANS FOR OUR BREAKOUT.
   I HAVE NEVER SEEN
MY INMATE COLLABORATOR;
   MAYBE I HEAR THINGS.
DO I WRITE DIALOGUE
   FOR BOTH VOICES?
AM I SOMEBODY'S ORACLE
   SERVING A SENTENCE?
THE DOOR WAS ALWAYS OPEN.

Epigrams

THE POETS OF ROME COME FROM VILLAGES THE SIZE OF
SULMO OR

SMALLER.
LOOKING BACK, EPIGRAMMATIC FORM LOOKS FORWARD
TO DORN, BORN

IN VILLA GROVE.

I DON'T READ M; I STUFF MYSELF AT HIS TABLE AND STILL LEAVE

HUNGRY.

WHEN I CAN'T UNDERSTAND ONE EPIGRAM, I EAT ANOTHER.

WHY IS IT THAT YOU NEVER WEAR THAT NECKLACE I STOLE FOR YOU?
NOBODY WILL GET SMART—ALL THE LOVE POETS STEAL FOR A LIVING.

DEBAUCHERY'S THE TREE WITH LONG LIMBS AND SHALLOW ROOTS.
THERE IS NO REST WITHIN ITS SHADE.

AFTER ALL THE ROLE REVERSALS AT SATURNALIA, LIFE PUTS
EVERYTHING BACK. ONLY WOMEN WEAR THE "SYNTHESIS."

AS IF TURPITUDE'S JUST GODS BEING FOLKS, AFTER ALL.

THE FIRST CAESAR INVENTED THE BULL FIGHT. THESEUS WAS THE
FIRST BULL FIGHTER. THE GREEKS INVENTED THESEUS.

THE ROMAN CROWDS INVENT THEMSELVES.

ARMOR, SWORD, AND SHIELD—FOR ALL THESE THINGS, DEATH IS
PUT OFF A LITTLE. (SENECA)

NO GLADIATOR'S LIKENESS WAS EVER STAMPED ON A COIN.

METAMORPHOSIS AS BURSTING THROUGH THE QUOTIDIAN INTO THE
DIVINE OR PERMANENT WORLD. (SURETTE)

READING *METAMORPHOSES* IS WALKING ON MOSAICS
THE LENGTH OF A PORTICO. AND BACK AGAIN.

I CANNOT SAY HOW I WROTE THIS. I AM SURE I COULD NEVER DO IT

AGAIN.

MY MIND BETRAYS ME LIKE SENATORS, SERVANTS, MISTRESSES, AND

SLAVES.

LAST NIGHT, WOLVES TOOK A VILLAGE CHILD.

THERE WILL BE A FUNERAL WITHOUT A BODY.

EVERYTHING ELSE SEEMS INCIDENTAL.

The Histories

AFTER THE FOREST WAS CUT CLEAR,
   THE TIBER FLOODED
TWELVE TIMES IN A SINGLE YEAR,
   NOTES LIVY,
REACHING THE MONUMENTS, SPREADING
   DISEASES,
AND CARRYING OFF CORPSES.
   ONLY
THE THICK WALLS OF THE HORREA
   SAVED THE GRAIN SUPPLY.
THE FIDENAE AMPHITHEATER
   COLLAPSED CLOSE BY,
AND THE RICH OPENED THEIR VILLAS
   TO THE VICTIMS
AMONG THE FIFTY THOUSAND INSIDE,
   CLAIMS TACITUS.
FOR ROME WAS BUILT ON A FLOODPLAIN.
   THIS FOR GOOD MEASURE:
"ROME WASN'T BUILT IN A DAY."
   VERGIL WROTE IT
FOR AUGUSTUS, TWO LINES A DAY.

The First Lesson is Listen

MY TEACHERS WHO HAVE PASSED ON
   REMAIN WITH ME
WHEN I THINK I AM MOST ALONE
   DECIDING WHICH WORD.
LATRO THE RHETORICIAN,
   NEITHER POET
NOR MUCH OF AN ORATOR,
   BUT ALL SPANISH MALE,

WOULD NOT LISTEN TO US DECLAIM
    OUR LAME ARGUMENTS,
CLAIMING INSTEAD STUDENTS MUST BE
    LISTENERS FIRST.
MESSALLA CENSURED PORCIUS
    LATRO THE ANGRY.
I HEAR HIM NOW THAT I LISTEN,
    BABY IOANNES.
TAKE TO HEART YOUR FATHER'S
    POSTHUMOUS POEMS.

Homer's Old Men on the Wall

IT'S NOW TIME I DESCRIBE THE CHANGE
    BEFORE I CAN'T.
IT'S NOT BIRTH EXACTLY, OLD AGE,
    OR DYING
(ALTHOUGH POETRY'S A SICKNESS
    NEARLY KILLED ME).
I SIMPLY ESCAPED THROUGH THE SPLIT
    DOWN MY BACK.
ALL SUMMER, I'VE FELT SOMETHING NEW
    HAPPENING.
I KNOW A THING FOR A DAY BUT
    WRITING REMEMBERS.
AT LAST, THE NEW POEM IS DONE
    CONCERNING
RED-EYED CICADAS RETURN
    STUBBORNLY
CLINGING TO A LOG IN OUR WALL,
    MEN TOO OLD TO FIGHT,
THEY MAKE CRUSTY ORATORS,
    THE CRYPTIC HUSKS

WHO SAT ON THE SHELF OF TROY'S WALL
    AND CHATTERED
AS IF FROM A HIGH TREE
    IN SHADY WOODS,
OR MORTALS WHO OVERHEARD
    THE MUSES' SINGING
SO SEDUCTIVE THEY FORGOT TO EAT
    AND DIED,
LANGUISHED UNDERGROUND
    SEVEN YEARS,
ONLY TO BE REBORN—
    CICADA!
MUSICIAN OF THE PERFECT SHELL
    LEFT BEHIND,
REMAINING IN THE SHAPE OF FLOWN
    CICADA!
EVERY DETAIL IS EXACTING.
    I REALIZE
THAT SAME EXUVIA ONCE COVERED
    MINE EYES.
THE PURPLE DYE JUST FOR HIS HEM
    CRUSHED TEN THOUSAND
SEASHELLS, EACH THE SHAPE
    OF A TRUMPET.

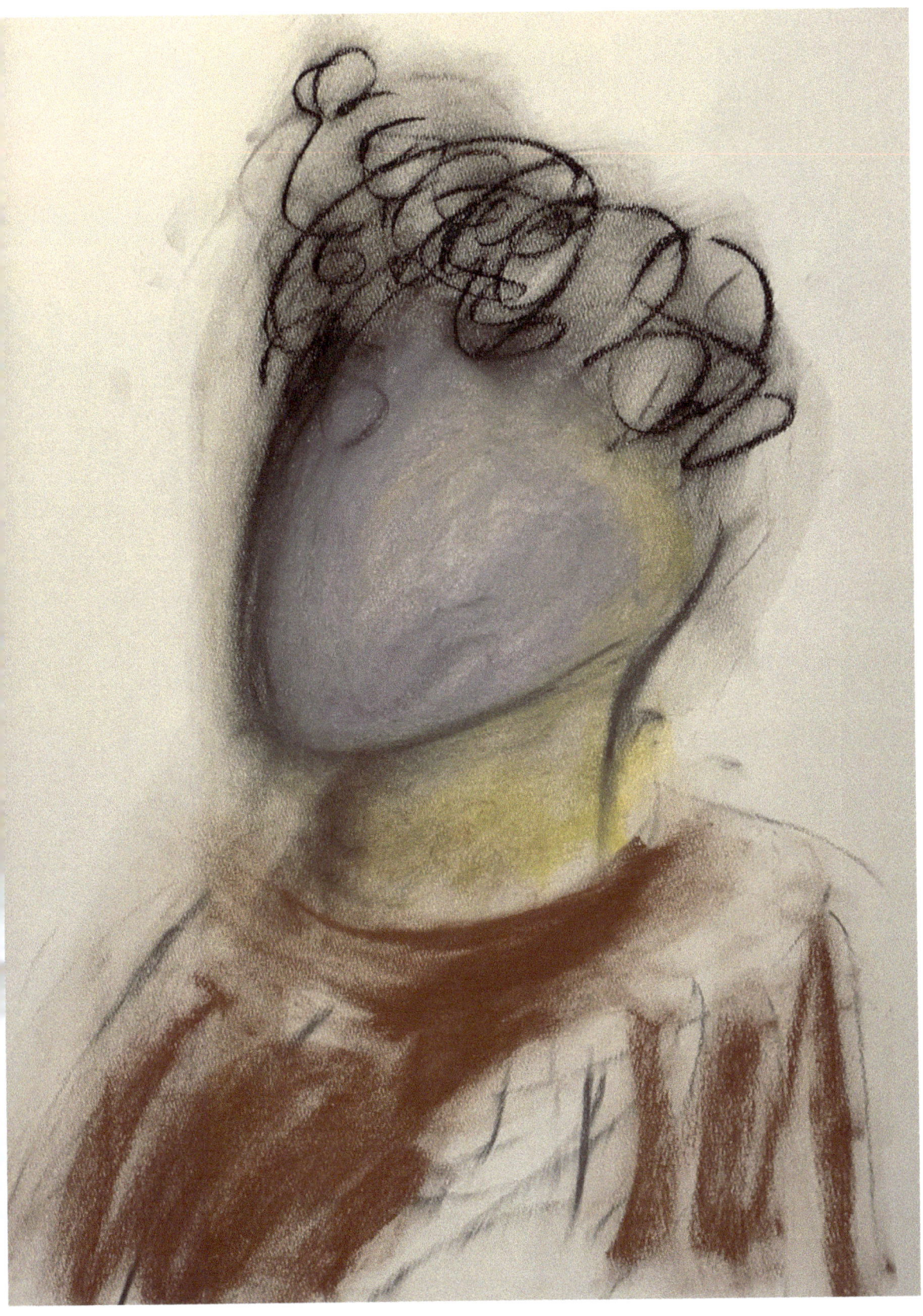

I Quit

I SOUND STRANGELY LIKE CATULLUS
    POST-*TRISTIA,*
AFTER THE LAST IMMORTALS PLED
    NOT GUILTY
OF RAPING MORTAL WOMEN,
    OBSTRUCTING JUSTICE,
FRAUD, MURDER, NEPOTISM,
    IDENTITY THEFT,
CORRUPTING FAMILIA VALUES,
    PUBLIC DRUNKENNESS,
CRUELTY TO ANIMALS,
    TRESPASS, INCEST,
ASSASSINATION, INSURRECTION,
    FALSE TESTIMONY,
HUBRIS AND BESTIALITY.
    HAVING EXHAUSTED
ALL APPEALS TO THE HIGHEST COURT,
    THE GODS SKIPPED BOND
NEVER TO BE HEARD FROM AGAIN.
    I QUIT WRITING
THE *METAMORPHOSES*
    AND REWRITING PROPERTIUS,
FOUND MYSELF A FRESH TOPIC
    FOR A NEW PURVIEW
ANNOUNCING THE CHANGES INSIDE
    A POET IN A WORLD
OF COMMODITY.
    "CIMBRORUMQUE
MINAS ET BENEFACTA
    MARI."

Everything Vibrates

THIS IS THE MORNING OF PERFECT
    DISTRACTION—
A PACKET OF LETTERS BARGES IN,
    ON TOP OF BUYING
A BRIDLE FOR THE NEW NAG.
    AH, WELL.
THE UNFINISHED SCROLL
    IS GOOD
FOR SCRATCHING MY BACK IN PLACES
    HARD TO REACH.

Dig

WHO DARES TAKE CARE OF MY OLD GARDEN?
    DON'T TRUST
THE TRANSLATORS TO DIG IT UP.
    PLEASE,
IF THE ROSALIAS ARE DEAD,
    DON'T REPLACE THEM.
THEY KNOW TO RETURN TO ASHES.

Digging Out

SENATORS, IGNORE YOUR RIVER
    AT ROME'S PERIL!
SEND IN ENGINEERS OR RISK
    TOMORROW WHEN SILT
THREE STORIES DEEP WILL SMOTHER
    INCREDULOUS STREETS,
AND WE'LL LIVE ON ROOFS AND CONSTRUCT
    BRIDGES BETWEEN DOORS!
OUR TREES SUBMERGED, THE CORSO
    RETURNED TO MUD.

Elpenor Unburied

I WAS ONE OF THE YOUNG JUDGES
    OVERSEEING
THE EXECUTION OF A MAN.
    THIS WAS
BEFORE I CONDEMNED MYSELF
    TO THE WRITER'S FATE.

(Believed to be) Ovid's Last Poem

ALL THIS TIME, I HAVE BEEN PRAYING
    TO THE WRONG GODS.
I'VE BEEN BURNING DOWN WHOLE FORESTS
    FOR INCENSE,
PILES OF FRANKINCENSE AND MYRRH
    ROSE LIKE SO MUCH SMOKE.
DRINKING KYKEON ONLY
    MADE ME THIRSTY.
I TRIED TO FIND MY CLINAMEN
    SOMEWHERE IN LUCRETIUS,
I SACRIFICED SLEEP,
    COLLECTED ITS BLOOD
AND BURNED THAT TOO.
    AT MY LOWEST POINT,
DON'T TELL, I EVEN TURNED TO
    WEARING TELINUM.
TAKE HEART FROM THE STORY.
    SCRIBONIA FLEW
TO JULIA, AFTER CAESAR
    TRANSFORMED HER
INTO THE GREAT LEOPARD MOTH.
    TWO MONTHS AGO,
TIBERIUS SENT THE LETTER…
    FLAVIA SAILS
TO SHARE THE HUT! I MUST PREPARE.

The Fourth Wall

THE FRESCO ON MY STUDY WALL
   DEPICTED
A STREET WOMAN SELLING CUPIDS.
   SHE SEEMED FAMILIAR,
A FIGURE I DREAMED OR PASSED BY
   REGULARLY,
NEVER BUYING ONE OF HER DOLLS.
   AND NOW
SHE OCCUPIES THE ROOM
   I WON'T SEE AGAIN,
WHERE ONCE I WROTE A POEM
   ABOUT HER.

Mosaics

IT IS POSSIBLE TO HAVE
   A POCKETFUL.
JULIUS CARRIED MOSAICS,
   SMALL EMBLEMATA,
WITH HIM INTO THE FIELD.

How to Make a Mosaic

WRITING POEMS WAS ALWAYS MORE
   LIKE A MOSAIC,
A TRICK TO PIECING TOGETHER
   TESSERAE,
   WORD PEBBLES
THAT PRESERVE THE ANCIENT STORIES
   MORE THAN PAINT.

The **Mosaic in the Floor**
THE MOON. A POOL. THE DRINKING HORSE.
   THE MOON MIRRORS
THE POOLING OF THE EVENING.
   REALIGNED,
THE HORSE HAS SWALLOWED HALF THE MOON.

The **Grand Mosaic** (Prelude for the Grand Collage)
THE FIGHT TO DEATH PRODUCED
   A CLEAR WINNER,
BUT THE FALLEN GLADIATOR,
   A RETARIUS,
MAIMED AND STILL BREATHING,
   WRITHES IN THE PUDDLE
   OF HIS OWN GORE.
HE ENTERED THE ARENA
   EQUIPPED WITH NET
   AND TRIDENT—
NO PLUMED HELMET INSCRIBED WITH MYTHS,
   NO SHIELD OR ARMOR,
NO SWORD, SHORT OR LONG, WITHOUT LANCE—
   MAIMED AND THROBBING,
IN THE CENTER OF EVERYTHING.
   EYES CAN'T TURN AWAY.
THE ANGRY CROWD SIGNALS THUMBS DOWN,
   BUT IBIS HAS LEFT
HIS BOX TO THE VESTAL VIRGINS
   STANDING BY PERPLEXED
AS TO WHY THE UNDERSTUDY
   IS NOT CALLED IN
TO DELIVER THE KILLING BLOW
   BETWEEN THE EYES?

TIBERIUS TAKES HIS PLACE,
    THEN TURNS HIS BACK TOO.
DEEP CUTS NOW EXPOSE WHAT SHOULD BE
    KEPT OUT OF SIGHT,
A WHOLE ANATOMY BENEATH
    FLAYED SKIN.
THE CHARMING POET HAS BECOME
    A PARACITE, LETCH,
A WHINING COMPLAINT, CAJOLER,
    TIRED SPECTACLE.
I, WHO ONCE PUZZLED TOGETHER
    THE GRAND MOSAIC
FROM ATOMS LUCRETIUS TOSSED ME
    TO PLAY WITH,
I PRAY FOR AN EASY DEATH.

Cutscene (after Christopher Neve)
HOMER TAKES MEN TO WAR AND BACK,
    BUT OVID'S JOURNEY
RISKS BOTH LOVE AND SEPARATION.
    HER THIGHS OPEN,
A FRESH WAX TABLET FOR LATE STYLE.
    WITHOUT CHARACTER,
THERE IS ONLY CONFUSION
    AND COCKALORUM.
THE POETS CANNOT WRITE WITHOUT
    WAR OR LOVE.
FOR THE MOSAIC IS MISSING
    MANY PIECES,
CAUSING THE DECLINING POET
    TO TAKE RISKS.
WRITING TAKES A LOT OUT OF HIM.

HE FEELS HIS AGE

FROM THE INSIDE NOW, MORE ANXIOUS

  THAN EVER

JUST TO FINISH, IF NOT POLISH

  THE FINISH.

TELLING THE BEES, HE RUNS AHEAD

  BEYOND HIS READER,

BEYOND HIS OWN UNDERSTANDING.

  HE'D BEEN WRONG:

MYTHS NEVER CHANGE; THEY TRANSFORM US.

  THE POEMS WERE NEVER

ABOUT MYTHS; EVERYTHING HE WROTE

  BECAME POETRY.

EACH PEBBLE SEEMED TO PLACE ITSELF,

  SO THE MOSAIC

CAME INTO BEING TO PICTURE

  A BUGONIA,

TO EMPTY THE MIND OF WORDS

  BEFORE SLEEP,

THE ROTTING CARCASS THAT CREATES

  HONEY BEES.

EACH NEW DAY, THE PICTURES TOLD MORE.

  NOW I SEE

THEY ARE GOING SOMEWHERE AHEAD OF ME

  ALWAYS OPENING.

THAT ACCOMPLISHED BEE MIGHT WELL DO

  FOR ANOTHER TALE,

AND LINKING THEM EXPANDS THE FLOOR

  YET ANOTHER TIME.

TO WAKE AND SEE THE FLOOR ANEW

  IS GOOD WORK.

Two-Fingered Exercise

WORD OF YOUR DIVORCE HAS REACHED HERE.

    BELIEVE ME,

NO FATHER WAS EVER CLOSER,

    OR MORE REMOVED,

THAN ME TO YOU FOR THOSE YEARS.

    WARS EAT UP MONEY.

LET YOUR CHILDREN HEAR HOW GOOD

    THEIR MOTHER IS.

BE SURE TO KEEP THE PROPER FACE.

    THEY WILL LOVE VISITS

AND SLEEPING OVER MOSAICS

    IN THEIR NEW BEDS,

KNOWING YOU ARE IN THE SPARE ROOM

    PRACTICING

THE FOUR-STRINGED PANDERA, THE GREAT,

    GREAT, GREAT, GREAT, GREAT, GREAT,

GREAT, GREAT, GREAT, GREAT, GREAT, GREAT, GREAT, GREAT,

    GREAT, GREAT, GREAT, GREAT, GREAT,

GREAT, GREAT, GREAT, GREAT, GREAT, GREAT, GREAT, GREAT,

    GREAT, GREAT, GREAT, GREAT, GREAT,

GREAT, GREAT, GREAT, GREAT, GREAT, GREAT, GREAT, GREAT,

    GREAT, GREAT, GREAT, GREAT, GREAT,

GREAT, GREAT, GREAT, GREAT, GREAT, GREAT, GREAT, GREAT,

    GREAT, GREAT, GREAT, GREAT, GREAT,

GREAT-GRANDFATHER TO THE GUITAR.

Out of the Running

SO THIS IS HOW IT WILL BE,
   MY MIND RACING LAPS.
AROUND MY BODY THE SPINA
   OUT OF IT
IN THE MIDDLE OF THINGS—
   THE STOLEN OBELISH
THRUST BESIDE ME LIKE A SPEAR
   IN THE SAND
CONNECTS THE COSMOS TO THE LAND—
   GOSSIP FLIES UP,
OFFFERINGS TO THE DIETIES
   OF SWIRLING RACES!
OLD LEGS GET UP CONSTANTLY
   TO PEE BETWEEN EGGS—
THE DUCTS THE GODS ENGINEERED
   BRING TEARS TO HER EYES,
LEAVING TRACKS DOWN HER MAKEUP,
   AS I ASK THE DRUNKS
WHO WON?

Mensis Septimus
MMXXIII

Bibliographia

Gregory S. Aldrete, *Floods of the Tiber in Ancient Rome*, 2006.

Hermann Bloch, *The Death of Virgil*, trans. Jean Starr Untermeyer, 1945.

Jacek Bocheński, *Naso the Poet*, trans. Tom Pinch, 2023.

The Cambridge Companion to Ovid, ed. Philip Hardie, 2002.

Mircea Cărtărescu, *Solenoid*, trans. Sean Cotter, 2022.

C.P. Cavafy, *Collected Poems*, trans. Edmund Keeley and Philip Sherrard, 1992.

Jo-Marie Claassen, *Ovid Revised: The Poet in Exile*, 2008.

Margherita Cole, "Ancient Scythian Shoe Preserved for 2,300 Years," My Modern MET, online, June 25, 2020.

Robert Duncan, "The Song of the Borderguard," *A Book of Resemblances*, 1966.

Epicurus: The Art of Happiness, trans. George K. Strodach, 2012.

Gilbert Highet, *Poets in a Landscape*, 1957.

Niklas Holzberg, *Ovid: The Poet and His Work*, trans. G.M. Goshgarian, 1998.

Jordanes, *The Origin and Deeds of the Goths*, trans. Charles C. Mierow, 2019.

David Malouf, *An Imaginary Life*, 1978.

Diane Middlebrook, *Young Ovid*, 2014.

Michael J. Mordine, "*Sine Me, Liber, Ibis*: The Poet, the Book and the Reader in *Tristia* I.1," online, November 19, 2010.

Christopher Neve, *Immortal Thoughts: Late Style in a Time of Plague*, 2023.

Ovid: The Erotic Poems, trans. Peter Green, 1983.

Ovid Metamorphoses, trans. Charles Martin, 2004.

Ovid: The Poems of Exile, trans. Peter Green, 2005.

Ovid's Poetry of Exile, trans. Joseph Skvorecky, 1990.

Tony Perrottet, *Route 66 A.D.*, 2002.

Ezra Pound, "Homage to Sextus Propertius," 1919.

Adrian Rădulescu, *Ovid in Exile*, 2019.

Sarah Ruden, *Vergil: The Poet's Life*, 2023.

Edward Said, *On Late Style*, 2006.

Joseph Skvorecky, *An Inexplicable Story*, trans. Káča Poláčková Henley, 2002.

Seutonius, *The Lives of the twelve Caesars: To which are added, His Lives of Grammarians, Rhetoricians, and Poets,* trans. Alexander Thompson, 2022.

Leon Surette, *A Light from Eleusis: A Study of Ezra Pound's Cantos*, 2000.

The Complete Poems of Tibullus, trans. Rodney G. Dennis and Michael C.J. Putnam, 2012.

Gareth Williams, *The Curse of Exile: A Study of Ovid's* Ibis, online April 12, 2006.

John Williams, *Augustus*, 1972.

David Wishart, *Ovid*, 2016.